PRAISE FOR UNBROKEN

In *Unbroken*, Goth combines the power of intention, personal experience, and professional training to create an action-oriented roadmap for healing sexual assault. More than a meditation on overcoming trauma, Goth's book provides a practical how-to guide for once again (or for the first time) feeling good in your body, mind, and heart.

— MICHELE ROSENTHAL, TRAUMA RECOVERY
SPECIALIST, AUTHOR OF *YOUR LIFE AFTER
TRAUMA: POWERFUL PRACTICES TO RECLAIM
YOUR IDENTITY*

Offering survivors practical tools with a warm and reassuring tone, Dr. Lesley Goth tackles the complicated issues of how to heal from sexual assault, combining firsthand experience with her expertise and skills as a psychologist. A beautiful resource for healing trauma.

— CHERYL ARUTT, PSY.D., AUTHOR OF *HEALING
TOGETHER: A PROGRAM FOR COUPLES*

Dr. Goth's personal experience with sexual assault, combined with her many years of helping those affected by it, are showcased in this guide to healing... her compassion for victims and knowledge of how to feel safe again is exemplified in her road to recovery manual.

— DANIELLE SCHREIBER, MEDICAL SALES
VISIONARY OWNER OF LEXIMED LLC

Lesley shines a light on all the guilt, shame, and self-blame I've carried because of my past. Her beautiful vulnerability, real-life stories from clients, and the affirmations and exercises show me that my feelings and actions of and for the past are shared by others who have had devastating experiences like mine. Thank you for such a fantastic book!

— ANGALA M. CRAMER, AUTHOR OF *INTERSOUL TRIBE: MAKING PEACE WITH YOUR INNER CRITIC, INNER CHILD, AND INNER WISDOM*

UNBROKEN

A Survivor's Journey After Sexual Assault

LESLEY GOTH, PSYD.

Red Thread Publishing LLC. 2025

Write to **info@redthreadbooks.com** if you are interested in publishing with Red Thread Publishing. Learn more about publications or foreign rights acquisitions of our catalog of books: www.redthreadbooks.com

Paperback ISBN: 979-8-89294-029-0

Ebook ISBN: 979-8-89294-028-3

Cover Design: Red Thread Designs

CONTENTS

DEDICATION

I dedicate this book to all the survivors of sexual assault. You have endured unimaginable challenges and yet remain standing strong. Your bravery, resilience, and trust in me are gifts I hold with the utmost respect. Each day that I have the privilege to do this work is an honor.

You share your stories with vulnerability and courage, and I want to honor you and your journey in the pages that follow. Here's to you and your path of healing.

INTRODUCTION

Welcome to the beginning of your journey to recovery. I want to share with you why I decided to author this book and give you an idea of what to expect. If you're reading this, likely, either you or someone you know has been through the trauma of sexual assault, and my heart goes out to you for that pain. It might sound cliché, but knowing you're not alone is essential.

Sexual assault is a devastating experience that impacts millions of individuals worldwide, leading to significant physical, emotional, and psychological challenges on the path to healing. Statistics show that one in three women and one in six men have faced sexual violence at some point in their lives. These numbers emphasize the urgent need for awareness, prevention, and support for survivors who often carry a heavy burden of shame.

You can feel the effects of sexual assault regardless of race, gender, or age. Over my 20 years as a trauma specialist working with survivors, I've seen shame and self-blame hinder the healing process for many. Having experienced assaults myself, including by someone I trusted, my goal is to offer hope and guidance towards overcoming these feelings of brokenness.

My personal experiences include instances of unwanted physical contact, being reduced to an object for someone else's sexual gratification, and enduring physical assault. My lack of consent was often disregarded, manipulated, or coerced. These encounters, coupled with the pervasive societal sexualization of women, instilled in me from a young age the belief that my body was merely a means to receive affection. I struggled to establish boundaries, frequently engaged in people-pleasing behaviors, and battled a destructive relationship with food and body image for years. I came to believe that the only way to feel lovable was through sexual interactions.

Like myself, you may be experiencing feelings of brokenness, lasting harm, or a sense of worthlessness as a result of past sexual assault(s). Survivors often grapple with emotions such as depression, anxiety, and utter despair. In addition, creating strong and healthy boundaries can be challenging for people who have gone through sexual assault, leaving them more vulnerable to toxic or abusive relationships. This book addresses boundaries to help you, as the survivor, learn to build trust and feel safe in relationships and society.

Through shared experiences and guidance on understanding shame and self-blame barriers, along with insights into the healing process, I aim to instill belief in the possibility of recovery. Why is it crucial to confront feelings of shame and self-blame? Firstly, every survivor grapples with these emotions, and secondly, until they are acknowledged and processed, the healing journey remains hindered, leaving one mired in the aftermath of their experiences. One of my clients bravely confronted her shame and self-blame, ultimately discovering the freedom to explore the deep-seated righteous anger she felt about her experiences. Here's what she recently shared with me:

> *I feel significantly better. I've been focusing on releasing the shame and guilt, realizing that I had overlooked the violation I experienced. Each morning, instead of acknowledging my violation, I was preoccupied with fears about being a terrible person and concerned about my partner's perception. It has taken a year to reach this point, and I'm furious that someone violated my*

body. The anger I feel now is immense; he exploited my body. Society often shifts blame onto victims while crediting the perpetrators—even allowing them into positions of power. I have learned to establish my sense of safety, which has made me feel much more empowered; it's as if I have lifted a tremendous burden.

Working through her feelings of shame and guilt was pivotal in initiating her healing journey. By releasing these burdens, she found the opportunity to heal and regain her strength. It is important to note that delving into sensitive topics such as shame and reading about others' experiences can elicit strong emotional responses, i.e., you may feel triggered. The exercises provided after each chapter aim to promote a sense of safety, self-compassion, and self-care while facilitating the healing process.

It is highly advisable to undertake specific exercises under the guidance of a trauma specialist to minimize any potential feelings of instability, triggering, or excessive vulnerability during your healing journey. Prioritizing safety is paramount in this process. All of the exercises presented in this book are designed to help you regulate your emotions, feel safe in your own skin, and regain a sense of normalcy.

This book offers valuable insights for both men and women. Men often confront unique challenges related to shame, which can be even more pronounced due to societal expectations that dictate they must embody strength, toughness, and resilience in the face of adversity. These pressures can complicate their healing journey after experiencing sexual assault, making it crucial for them to find support and understanding.

Each chapter will delve into everyday struggles and questions survivors face, with educational content aimed at empowering you with knowledge. I will interweave real-life examples from myself and other survivors alongside compassionate practical exercises and positive affirmations designed to kickstart your healing journey and illuminate the path ahead. I won't use real names or specific client details in shared stories. Instead, they'll be a blend of various clients and situations.

A TikTok video I created, in which I openly shared my experience of surviving sexual assault at the hands of known individuals, sparked the inspiration for this book. The outpouring of responses I received from this video highlighted the urgent demand for resources to support individuals like yourself in navigating through such traumatic experiences. I have brought this book to life by leveraging my profound expertise as a licensed clinical psychologist specializing in PTSD, C-PTSD, eating disorders, anxiety, and depression for over two decades.

I've listened to your stories; I've felt your pain.

My ultimate goal behind authoring this book is education, encouragement, and inspiration—to empower you as the reader by offering valuable information and practical advice on navigating life after sexual assault while fostering hope throughout your healing process. In this book, you will learn that these events do not define you; your voice and experiences matter. Are you supporting a loved one who has experienced sexual assault? If so, a dedicated section is included at the end to offer guidance on providing optimal support and care.

I encourage you to approach each chapter based on what resonates most with your needs—whether taking them individually as standalone guides or reading through the entire book—because everyone's journey is unique. Your empowerment begins as you reflect on what support means during this healing time.

I promise healing is possible; no one must face this journey alone. I am excited to embark on this process with you.

As you begin this adventure of healing, keep an open mind. Embrace new perspectives, rediscover yourself, and embrace self-love to break free from the past. It's fundamental to at least be willing to release any shame or self-blame. Remember to have a journal handy for the exercises at the end of each chapter. Recording your journey will allow you to track your progress and appreciate how much you've grown. Some of the exercises may sometimes feel repetitive, but trust me, that is because they are essential and valuable to your sense of safety and foundation for further healing.

Regarding the affirmations at the end of each chapter, please do not skip over them. Affirmations are powerful ways to rewire your brain and shift your mindset towards positivity and healing. When you repeat affirmations (I recommend at least a minute per day, but feel free to go longer!), you create new neural pathways reinforcing powerful beliefs and mindsets. Affirmations boost confidence, reduce stress, reduce negative beliefs, and improve overall well-being.

You will have a few affirmations, so pick the one that resonates most with you at the time. You can choose a different one depending on your feelings and needs later. Also, feel free to adjust the wording so that the affirmation resonates with who you are.

The final chapter contains all the definitions related to sexual assault. You can revisit this chapter whenever you need clarification on specific terms associated with sexual assault. All the definitions are clearly outlined for your reference as needed.

Here is an exercise to set the foundation of safety and knowing how to care for yourself as you begin your journey.

EXERCISE

In your journey towards healing, it is crucial to understand how to soothe your inner turmoil when faced with triggering situations. Begin by embracing these indispensable techniques that foster a sense of safety within yourself. These techniques empower you to acknowledge past experiences, share your desired narrative, and nurture your well-being. These safety tools are foundational for the chapters ahead, especially since much of the content can be triggering.

1. **Mindful Container:** Envision a substantial container in your mind, equipped with a prominent lock to safeguard its contents. Let your imagination run wild - whether it resembles a fortified vault, a secure storage unit, or even an impregnable prison cell. Customize its dimensions, hues, and security features according to your preferences. When overwhelmed by unsettling emotions or thoughts – what I like to call

moments of "angst" — entrust them to your mental container for safekeeping. Lock away this angst until you are ready and supported enough to confront and address it. I utilize my container before commencing my day with clients; locking away any inner turmoil allows me to focus on their needs effectively. By day's end, I retrieve my emotions from the container and determine the necessary steps for self-care — be it confiding in a therapist, sharing with a friend, or pouring thoughts into a journal.

2. **Sacred Haven:** Once more, delving into the realms of imagination, visualize a serene sanctuary that either exists or materializes solely within your mind. This safe space could mirror a cherished location from past travels or be an entirely new creation designed to evoke tranquility and serenity. Engage all five senses as you immerse yourself in this haven — envisioning sights, smells, sounds, tastes, and textures that bring comfort. Take slow, deep breaths to anchor yourself in this special place, allowing relaxation to wash over you and granting solace to your body amidst calmness and peace.

Embrace these practices as pillars of strength on your path toward healing; hone the ability to navigate triggers with grace while nurturing inner tranquility and resilience. Various techniques exist to assist in calming the nervous system during trauma recovery, including deep breathing, mindfulness practices, progressive muscle relaxation, and grounding exercises. These methods aid in regulating the body's stress response and fostering a sense of security and tranquility essential for trauma recovery. The chapters go further into these exercises so that by the end of the book, you will feel like your toolbox is complete!

AFFIRMATIONS

Here are some affirmations to get you started. Remember to pick or develop one that resonates with you the most now, and let's begin!

I deserve to heal and feel better.

Everything will be okay, even if I don't feel like it now.

It would be okay if all I did today was breathe.

Chapter One

IS IT MY FAULT?

Hold yourself back or heal yourself back together.

— BRITTANY BURGURDER

I had a few drinks, showered, then headed to my neighbor's place. We partied, smoked some weed, and kept the drinks flowing. All I recall is mentioning that I should leave. The next morning, I woke up with fuzzy memories. He claims I suggested having sex, but I can't recollect that part. He was upset that I didn't remember and couldn't grasp why I felt so uneasy and distressed. Maybe I shouldn't have consumed so much alcohol. Why did I even decide to go over there? What if I had just stayed home chilling with my dog? How did things escalate to us having sex? Maybe it's on me for this mess, and now I feel dirty and ashamed. He insists it's my fault, and sadly, I have no choice but to trust his narrative.

I s there any part of this story that resonates? This young woman was overwhelmed by shame and self-blame for what happened at her neighbor's apartment. You may read her words and find yourself blaming her as well! After all, it is so easy to blame the victim especially if she had been drinking. However, drinking or being under the influence NEVER gives anyone the right to have sex with you. It is this negative belief system that complicates the traumatic event(s) and causes you to feel so stuck in your healing. So, let's delve into the challenging topic of survivors' guilt, shame, and self-blame, particularly prevalent among sexual assault survivors.

I recently had a conversation with a client who believed her involvement with her 36-year-old boss at 16 was entirely her fault. She constantly criticized herself for not voicing her concerns, allowing the situation to persist for an extended period, and not ending it sooner. Despite the reality that she was still a minor, he was the adult, her superior, and a trusted authority figure, she continued to struggle with the idea that he may have manipulated her and that she was, in fact, a victim of severe, repeated sexual assault. When her mother discovered what had happened, she reacted violently by beating her and sending her to her room. Later in her life, upon sharing this experience with her husband, he similarly placed blame on her, resorting to calling her derogatory names such as "whore" and other highly damaging terms.

The feelings of shame and blame imposed by her mother and husband perpetuated the belief that she was at fault. However, through counseling and talk therapy, alongside experiencing compassion that had previously eluded her, she began to reevaluate her situation. By considering how she would view this scenario if it involved her teenage grandchildren, she ultimately recognized that she had been groomed by her employer, manipulated, and sexually exploited; thus, it was not her fault. Releasing this self-blame was life changing for her. She had carried this burden of guilt and shame for over 50 years.

Through two decades of experience, I have repeatedly observed how these emotions hinder individuals as they attempt to progress in their healing journeys. The repercussions of sexual assault are profound, compounded by the burdens of shame and blame that survivors often bear. This dual impact is not only distressing but also crippling, which underscores the significance of this book in your healing process. By the end of this chapter, you will have effectively begun to alleviate the hold of shame and self-blame on your spirit.

Let's start by addressing the confusion and letdown you might feel about how your body reacted during your sexual assault. Your response to trauma can lead to feelings of guilt and self-reproach. Questions like, "Why didn't I escape?", "Why did I freeze instead of speaking up?", or like the above client, "Why did I let it go on for so long?" are common and feed the belief that what happened is your fault. What I am hoping to help you understand is that the complexity of trauma responses (whether you froze or fled) further complicates self-blame since our bodies react instinctively during survival mode. Our brain's priority during trauma is survival through fight, flight, freeze, or fawn reactions.

Instead of being upset at your trauma response, what would it be like to honor it? If you freeze and are upset about freezing and not fighting back, maybe you can start to appreciate that your body did what it needed to do to survive.

Acknowledging and respecting your innate survival instincts that guided you through crises is imperative. Recognizing the body's drive for survival can be empowering instead of faulting yourself for not reacting differently later on. Each person's trauma journey is unique due to circumstances beyond their control. The lesson learned is to trust your body's instincts for protection instead of criticizing yourself for doing what was necessary for your safety.

The individual discussed in this chapter exemplifies the fawn response. She conformed and sought to appease others, engaging in people-pleasing behaviors to evade suffering and retribution. Her struggle with the prolonged nature of her situation becomes more apparent as we examine her fawning defense mechanism. Not only did she derive feelings of uniqueness from her abuser, who manipulated her, but she also recognized that confiding in her mother would likely result in blame and shame, similar to the reaction she received when the truth eventually came to light. Given that she felt unsafe disclosing what was occurring, what could she do? She felt trapped in a no-win scenario, and her fawning response offered a temporary shield against pain and humiliation. Through her therapy, she gained a deeper understanding of this dynamic, learned to forgive herself for the self-blame, and recognized the importance of her survival.

Another client I collaborated with experienced significant shame regarding her freeze response. She had always perceived herself as a strong, self-advocating, and powerful woman. It was difficult for her to wrap her brain around why she had frozen during the attack. However, through her EMDR therapy (which I will explain further later), she came to view her freezing response as a protective mechanism rather than a negative trait. I like to frame it as a gift, not a curse. Here is what she shared after this realization:

> *I could have prevented this, but also made it much worse. I usually stand up to bullies, so why didn't I use my voice? Why would I freeze? I'm trying to prove to myself that my trauma response was legit. It is legit!! Do you know why? Because I'm still here. Freezing was "doing" something. My body knew what to do, and it protected me!*

Next comes the relentless cycle of tormenting questions that invade your thoughts, centered around the unending "what if" scenarios. Addressing these "what if" inquiries, which contribute to your feelings of shame and self-reproach, is a significant milestone in overcoming self-doubt and self-loathing during the healing journey.

Do you often say, "What if" and then fill in the blank? This type of question is about your brain trying to get back a sense of control that gets stripped away during traumatic events. When you realize that trauma can make you feel like you've lost control and safety, your brain will kick into gear trying to figure things out to regain that sense of security. My client says, *"The 'What if' helps me avoid feeling so helpless. If I can see what I did wrong, then I can control it for the next time. The reality is you can't control everything, and I need to be ok with that".*

Our brains crave balance and closure. Even if it lands on the idea that it was your fault, at least it's some explanation. But deep down, you know it's just not right and won't bring the relief you're after. Let's look at the examples I hear from survivors all the time:

- *"What if I hadn't had those drinks that night?"*
- *"What if I hadn't accepted that ride?"*
- *"What if I'd skipped my evening run?"*
- *"What if I'd pushed him away?"*
- *"What if I hadn't been so friendly?"*
- *"What if I'd chosen a different outfit?"*
- *"What if I hadn't frozen?"*

What are the "what if" questions that you find yourself contemplating? I am aware they exist because every survivor grapples with them. My questions included: *"What if I hadn't spent the night at my friend's house and allowed her older brother to 'play' with us?"* Or, *"What if I had not been wearing headphones and could have heard my attacker approaching from behind?"* Additionally, *"What if I had simply said 'no' to my date and not invited him into my home, preventing him from taking advantage of me? Why didn't I just refuse?"*

I have carried those questions and the accompanying shame for many years. Looking back, the feelings of torment and self-loathing are deeply distressing. I understand that you may share similar emotions, so we must confront these feelings and finally put them to rest. The exercises outlined below significantly aided me in reframing my "what ifs," allowing me to release the shame and self-blame I had been holding onto. I assure you that you can achieve this, too, and it is perfectly acceptable to move beyond what has been preventing you from letting go of those burdens. Below is the feedback I received from my client after completing these exercises:

> *The experience I had of being drugged is intricately linked to shame over my alcohol consumption, creating a complex and confusing situation. I frequently find myself attributing blame to my drinking that night. However, I have come to realize the*

importance of examining my symptoms, trusting my instincts, and acknowledging that, regardless of my drinking, it does not excuse anyone's decision to drug and harm me.

Engage with the exercises and affirmations to free yourself from what no longer benefits you. Remember that you've already been through enough. You deserve to let this go and be free!

EXERCISES

By reshaping negative beliefs about past traumas through introspection and reframing them externally, you can nurture self-compassion and empathy towards your own experiences. Transitioning from contemplating "what if" scenarios to acknowledging "what is/was" directs attention towards factual information rather than hypothetical possibilities. The goal is to stay grounded in reality. You cannot alter the past; our focus should be on treating ourselves with compassion for our past choices. If you had been aware of impending adverse outcomes, you would have decided differently to avoid putting yourself in harm's way.

If the exercises below feel triggering, please pause and either return to the introduction exercises and do those again or bring them to your therapist, who can support and guide you through them.

1. Make a list of all the "what ifs" that plague you.

2. Then, make another list of the "what is/was" facts from your sexual assault. For example, *"What if I didn't flirt with him at the bar?"*. Change that to *"I did flirt, but that was not consent to have sex with me or touch me in a way that made me uncomfortable."* Do you notice the difference and how this feels in your body vs perseverating on "what if"?

3. Next, I want you to start imagining how you'd support a friend in a similar situation. *What would you tell them? Would you blame them as you blame yourself? Or would you comfort, support, and help*

them see it was not their fault? Write down a script of what you would tell your friend. Then, read those same responses to yourself. This exercise can help reshape your self-image positively.

These exercises aim to invoke introspection while reframing negative beliefs surrounding past traumas. By examining how we blame ourselves and questioning these narratives from an external perspective, you can foster self-compassion and empathy towards your own experiences. Considering how you would support a friend sharing a similar story can offer valuable insight into reshaping your self-perception. Ultimately, embracing a narrative acknowledging the true nature of what occurred while releasing unfounded guilt allows for genuine healing and self-acceptance.

AFFIRMATIONS

These empowering affirmations encourage acknowledging that you can release any feelings of shame and self-blame associated with your past experiences. You can relinquish unwarranted blame and redirect it to its rightful place, i.e., the perpetrator. Pick your affirmations for today, and remember you can switch them up as needed. Feel empowered to personalize the wording to resonate more authentically with you if necessary.

I acknowledge that I can release shame or blame from my past experiences.

I can release feelings of guilt and hold the proper people responsible.

Understanding that what occurred was not my responsibility paves the way for healing and liberation from unnecessary self-blame.

Chapter Two

WHAT IF I GAVE CONSENT?

Always remember, if you have been diagnosed with PTSD, it is not a sign of weakness; rather, it's proof of your strength because you have survived!

— MICHEL TEMPLET

What if I said, 'ok' because I was scared and felt like I had no other option? I don't know how to forgive myself for this.

I was so afraid of upsetting him, so I gave in.

I realize I said 'yes,' but my body said 'no.'

These women shared their experiences of feeling compelled to give consent out of fear or pressure, leading to a sense of self-blame. They struggled with the conflict between their verbal agreement and true feelings when they felt coerced, pressured, or threatened into compliance.

I remember after my divorce when I started dating again, I was out on a second date and having a great time. I had been drinking and explicitly stated that I wasn't going to engage in sexual activity as my date drove me home. Despite repeatedly voicing my refusal once back home, I finally got too exhausted to keep saying no. My intoxicated state made me vulnerable and eventually led me to give in against my wishes. Looking back, I regret caving in; I grappled with feelings of guilt due to being drunk and blamed myself. I struggled with that issue for a long time and had to do the work I'm asking you to do now. I know I'm not alone when feeling like it was my fault since I ended up relenting and giving consent. Nevertheless, it clearly shows when people do not respect boundaries, lines get crossed.

One burning question that may be weighing on your mind is: *What if I agreed to it? Or, what if I didn't say "no"?* Let's delve into these questions and navigate the complexities of consent in the context of survivors' experiences so that you can once and for all relieve yourself of this burden.

To start, what does consent even mean? It's about giving permission, being aware, and being able to agree to something that you're comfortable with. It signifies your willingness, competence, sound judgment, and agreement to whatever you propose. Many people do not know that individuals must give consent freely and they can withdraw it at any moment. Without consent, any sexual activity is considered assault, no matter the relationship between the people involved. Consent is both verbal and nonverbal.

In addition, consenting to certain sexual activities does not imply consent for all behaviors. Individuals can be comfortable with some actions but not others. For instance, a partner may engage in unacceptable conduct, such as removing a condom without permission, even if previous acts were consensual. I want to be clear that consent for specific actions does not equate to blanket consent across all situations.

In an ideal, intimate, non-assault interaction, if you gave consent, it indicates that you were okay with it at that time. Your body and mind were in alignment and readily engaged.

What if you didn't agree to it? Or, what if you said yes but didn't feel right or weren't in the right mind? Sometimes, what we say out loud doesn't match how we truly feel inside. I hear from women who said yes with their words, but their bodies said no. There could be various reasons for that – like fear of being hurt, fear of being left alone, fear of feeling embarrassed, fear of upsetting another person, and more.

> *At first, I felt at ease sitting on his lap, enjoying our playful banter and fun. We exchanged a few kisses, and before I knew it, we were on my bed, where he started to remove my clothing. At first, I laughed and felt comfortable, but soon an unsettling feeling washed over me, and I voiced my discomfort. Unfortunately, he responded by restraining my hands, and sadly, the rest is history.*

Here's the truth – it wasn't your fault, even if you said yes initially. You gave consent when you felt comfortable with the situation; however, when things changed and you withdrew your approval by saying no later, it showed that you were no longer at ease. You are not obligated to say why you changed your consent. All that matters is that you revoked permission. Anyone who respects you will adapt accordingly.

Remember this: You have every right to change your mind during any form of intimate or sexual encounter. There aren't any specific rules or laws that say you can't change your mind. If the other person doesn't respect your change in consent and pushes forward anyway, that's crossing a line into assault territory because they failed to acknowledge your boundaries.

Let's explore a situation where a "no" can change to a "yes" during intimate moments with someone. A "no" does not turn to a "yes" unless some form of pressure or manipulation is involved. As mentioned earlier in this chapter regarding my experience with my date, he continued to push forward after some drinks despite my discomfort and repeated refusals. He disregarded my boundaries! When your "no" is overlooked or trivialized, it often leads to the depreciation of your worries or the use of emotional coercion, such as threatening to end the relationship if you do not consent.

People can pressure you into changing your "no" to a "yes" in many ways – it's all about controlling the situation. Remember, "no" always means "no". If external factors influence you to alter your response to a "yes," chances are the person involved used some level of force or persuasion. And remember, that's not on you; it falls under the category of assault.

Was or is the person you're involved with showing blatant signs of disrespect by not honoring your boundaries? My date completely ignored my boundaries, and yours were most likely ignored, too. It's impossible to address every possible scenario concerning consent. Still, I hope you are getting a better idea of what it is and the key points you can give it or remove it anytime.

EXERCISE

Similar to what we discussed in the previous chapter, I encourage you to bring in some compassion toward any guilt or shame you might be carrying. Consider scenarios where you initially gave consent, withdrew, or maybe never gave it but later succumbed to pressure. If a dear friend shared a similar experience with you -- would you blame them for what happened? Extend that kindness to yourself. It wasn't your fault; someone violated your boundaries and silenced your voice, which is unacceptable.

Consider how you would react if someone close confided in you with such a story, and jot down those thoughts in your journal. Write down the supportive words you'd offer them, then redirect those affirmations toward yourself. If this was your experience, remember that it's not your fault that someone disregarded, disrespected, invalidated, and manipulated your boundaries for their benefit. Embrace tenderness, practice self-compassion, welcome it into your life, and notice how liberating it feels as you let go of the guilt, shame, and self-blame surrounding consent issues.

AFFIRMATIONS

These affirmations focus on your right to be human and change your mind. Repeat them and enjoy the soothing feeling of knowing you are learning, growing, and healing.

It is human to err, and I can show myself compassion knowing I did my best in a situation that caused me harm.

I am allowed to change my mind.

I can add context to past decisions that I'm not happy about.

Chapter Three

WHAT IF MY ABUSER WAS SOMEONE I TRUSTED?

You are not defined by your past. You are prepared by it.

— UNKNOWN

My family had been a part of this church for generations. It was supposed to be a place of safety, acceptance, and love. Instead, my pastor took advantage of me when I was just a child. He threatened to hurt my parents if I ever spoke up. He did unthinkable things to me, most of which I have blocked out from memory. He spent the holidays with us. He baptized me and my siblings. He was so much a part of our family, and what he did was incredibly damaging to my heart, soul, faith, and overall sense of safety in knowing who I can trust. It's time to heal and let this pain go, finally. I want to trust again. I want my life back.

Recovering from sexual assault or rape can feel incredibly overwhelming when someone you love or are closely connected to, such as a spouse, family member, mentor, or faith leader, is the perpetrator. It's not just about healing from the trauma; it's about navigating the complicated emotions that arise from having to set boundaries with someone who has been a significant part of your life. Understanding these dynamics can make the recovery process even more challenging as you grapple with the pain of betrayal while trying to reclaim your sense of safety and self.

I have experienced multiple instances of assault, the majority of which were perpetrated by individuals I was familiar with and had placed my trust in. Shockingly, research indicates that a significant proportion of sexual assaults are committed by someone the victim knows, as highlighted by the client's testimony above. Various studies and reports suggest that approximately 70% to 90% of sexual assault victims are attacked by someone they know, including acquaintances, friends, family members, or intimate partners. This statistic can vary based on the specific population studied and the definitions used in the research. However, it's important to note that these figures highlight the prevalence of sexual violence in familiar relationships, underscoring the complexities surrounding consent and trust.

Sexual assault by someone you know can be more brutal to recover from than assault by a stranger for several reasons:

1. **Betrayal of Trust:** When the perpetrator is someone known to you, it creates a profound feeling of betrayal and a breach of trust that hits the core of who you are. This betrayal trauma hinders the ability to trust others during the recovery journey.
2. **Feelings of Guilt and Self-blame:** Victims of sexual assault by someone you know may cause feelings of guilt, self-blame, and confusion about the relationship, which can hinder the healing process. Organically, it is easier to carry the burden of blame than wrap your brain around the reality that this person of trust could cause you harm in a heinous way. In doing so, the perpetrator can remain a safe attachment and person of trust and safety.
3. **Fear of Retaliation:** As the client shared at the beginning of this chapter, victims may fear retaliation or further harm from the perpetrator if they speak out, making it difficult to seek help and support.

4. **Complex Emotions:** The emotional impact of sexual assault by someone known can be more complex, as victims may have conflicting feelings of love, anger, and confusion towards the perpetrator. Sometimes, an individual may find it unsettling when a family member or significant other, who typically displays affection, support, and compassion, can also inflict harm. Attempts to rationalize their behavior by emphasizing their positive qualities can downplay the seriousness of the betrayal of trust and boundaries. It is crucial to recognize that kindness does not negate the potential for someone to exhibit monstrous behavior.

5. **Social Stigma and Shame:** There may be additional layers of shame and stigma associated with being assaulted by someone known, as victims may fear judgment or disbelief from others. In some cases, mainly when the offender is a respected figure like a coach or teacher, or when the assault involves individuals of the same gender, it can present significant challenges. For example, suppose an assault occurred between two men. In that case, there exists a societal expectation for men to exhibit strength and resilience, hence leading to feelings of shame and self-blame in instances of such assaults.

I have supported numerous clients who have experienced mistreatment from various family members, including fathers, brothers, cousins, grandfathers, and husbands, as well as from trusted individuals in positions of authority, such as coaches, teachers, and religious leaders. It requires time, patience, and a safe environment to navigate through the mixed emotions that are entirely valid and widespread. For instance, you may feel confusion and shame for feeling anger towards the individual while fearing the potential loss of that relationship. I promise those feelings are typical and expected.

Kids are often told by their abuser not to speak up about such experiences out of fear of repercussions within the family or not being believed. It can be conflicting and deeply confusing to see someone shift from being a protector to a predator, making it challenging to come to terms with. How is a child supposed to make sense of this? When the one supposed to keep you safe turns into causing harm, it throws off your entire nervous system and makes it hard to feel safe and secure or know who you can trust.

I believe my client articulates this succinctly:

> *When my parental figure inflicted harm, my mind attempted to convince me that it's safe and acceptable, while my body reacted by indicating that it isn't. Sometimes, the roles reverse; my body feels fine, but my mind insists that this cannot be alright. It's incredibly confusing and a total mind f*ck!*

One of the most troubling experiences of my childhood occurred when I was about three or four years old. Although the specifics are hazy, I vividly recall a profound sense of discomfort whenever I was near a particular family friend. He was a respected doctor in our community, someone who was supposed to care for me, yet I believe he took advantage of a vulnerable child. I never spoke about this until now, fearing no one would believe me. At that age, I was unaware of what had transpired or how to articulate my feelings. I was simply too young and bewildered.

With my insights gained from this experience and the client's account in this chapter, being assaulted by someone who holds a position of trust or authority presents a complex and bewildering challenge. It resembles an internal tangle of emotions and thoughts. As noted by the client, when the perpetrator is a spiritual leader, it adds another challenging dimension that affects one's perception of God and faith. Victims often grapple with feelings of betrayal alongside confusion, anger, and profound spiritual disillusionment. They may also contend with guilt, shame, and uncertainty regarding their beliefs—especially when faced with the troubling idea that an individual who represents God's authority could commit such a dreadful act. The question arises: if God embodies love, how can such occurrences be allowed? Many individuals might feel forsaken or punished by God, resulting in a significant spiritual crisis and estrangement from their faith community.

As a survivor, you must seek support from trained professionals, such as therapists or counselors, who can help you navigate these complicated emotions and work towards healing. Rebuilding a sense of trust, safety, and spirituality may take time and involve re-evaluating your beliefs and finding new ways to connect with your faith on your terms.

Now, let's talk about when abuse is coming from a partner or spouse. Partner abuse, unfortunately, occurs more frequently than we realize. In this type of situation, there may be pressure to comply due to the relationship status, leading to confusion and difficulty processing the abuse. Let me be clear about something. Just because you are married does not mean consent no longer exists. It is a privilege to give your body to your partner. It is not your partner's right to have it. Religions might say differently, and some scriptures about women submitting to their husbands can be twisted and misused. It's a shame that this still happens today, even in more modern societies. Regardless, the minute you feel like your thoughts, feelings, and physical space aren't valued or respected, that's a significant warning sign, no matter your beliefs or relationship situation.

Maybe your abuser was not a spouse or family member but a friend or someone you have dated. Date rape is sadly a frequent occurrence. Sometimes, we might brush it off as not serious because we're familiar with the perpetrator and find it hard to believe they could hurt us. Other times, we downplay it out of shame and self-blame for finding ourselves in that situation in the first place. Many individuals often avoid labeling it as rape or sexual assault to avoid facing the harsh reality of the problem, which can be incredibly challenging. Denial acts as a significant defense mechanism in such experiences. When this happened to me on a second date, it was less daunting to minimize the assault than to face the genuine consequences of the trauma. The date and the ensuing events were far beyond what I had consented to. Rather than confronting the truth of what occurred, I continued to see him! Denial and gaslighting myself was my method of diminishing the situation's overall effect and involvement.

At times, you may find yourself trapped in a situation where you must stay near your abuser, such as when they are your co-workers or when you continue to see them at school or family events. Managing these distressing triggers while attempting to maintain relationships with those who have caused you harm is emotionally overwhelming. Survivors must seek support from trusted individuals, counselors, and support groups to navigate this healing process. It's ok to struggle with trusting others, even those who are professionals and trained to help. Take your time and go at your own pace. With dedication, perseverance, and commitment, you can navigate this sense of betrayal, let go of any guilt you may be holding onto, and discover how to establish healthy boundaries that ensure your safety. The following exercises facilitate this process for you.

EXERCISES

Here are some steps you can take to start the healing process.

1. **Create a safe space:** Set up a comfy spot at home or outdoors where you can relax. Consider lighting a candle, playing calming music, or enjoying a hot drink. Grab a blanket, your favorite cozy item, or a pillow, and make sure the atmosphere feels snug and secure.
2. **Acknowledge your feelings**: Take out your journal and allow yourself to write and feel the full range of emotions that come with betrayal, such as anger, sadness, and hurt. Don't try to suppress or ignore your feelings.
3. **Seek support**: Reach out to trusted friends, family members, or a therapist who can listen and offer emotional support. Talking about your feelings can help you process them and feel less alone.
4. **Set boundaries**: It's essential to protect yourself from further harm by setting boundaries with the person who betrayed you. Boundaries may involve limiting contact or ending the relationship altogether. More about boundaries in chapter 7.

5. **Practice self-care**: Take care of yourself physically, emotionally, and mentally. Engage in activities that bring you joy and relaxation, such as exercise, meditation, or spending time in nature.
6. **Forgiveness**: Consider whether forgiveness is a part of your healing process. Forgiveness does not mean condoning the betrayal but rather letting go of the negative emotions holding you back.
7. **Therapy**: Consider seeking treatment from a licensed therapist who specializes in trauma and betrayal. Therapy can provide tools and coping strategies to help you navigate your healing journey.

AFFIRMATIONS

These affirmations are specifically chosen to address the painful experience of being sexually assaulted by someone trusted. Some days may feel daunting, but I'm here to reassure you. You can do this!

I am allowed to be confused and struggle.

What happened to me does not define me, and I am learning to be free from shame and see my worth.

I don't need permission to exist. I can create my safety.

Chapter Four

WHAT IF I LIKED IT?

You are not alone. You are not to blame. You are worthy of healing.

— UNKNOWN

In therapy, I keep shutting down at a certain point in the process. I hit a wall. I know what happened to me was not my fault and that these people, these family members, took advantage of me and are very sick people. However, the wall hits whenever I remember feeling special, liking their attention, or my body liking it. Finding pleasure makes me feel so gross and nasty inside.

What if experiencing sexual assault elicited feelings of pleasure? I previously recounted an incident during a sleepover at a friend's house when her older brother wanted to join us. When it was time for bed, he climbed in with us and began touching us inappropriately. To be honest, I felt a conflicted sense of enjoyment. However, I was acutely aware that something was profoundly wrong. I experienced a deep sense of unease and felt violated, yet I struggled to understand why. I was so confused about how something could simultaneously feel so bad and so good.

This question is a hard one to reconcile, as you can imagine. I am here to tell you it is common for individuals, especially those who experienced childhood sexual trauma, to feel deep shame when grappling with this topic, hindering their ability to recover. For many, it's a complete roadblock to healing. You cannot address "What if I liked it?" without understanding how the body is wired at a basic scientific level.

The body's natural response to pleasure, even in everyday situations, involves the release of dopamine, a neurotransmitter closely linked to feelings of enjoyment. Activities such as savoring the aroma of freshly baked cookies or engaging in sexual intimacy stimulate dopamine release in the brain, reinforcing and enhancing pleasurable experiences.

Another neurotransmitter, serotonin, is linked to feelings of happiness and is often found at lower levels in individuals dealing with depression. Research has shown that touch and sexual intimacy are intensely pleasurable experiences for both humans and animals. Harry Harlow's study on monkeys revealed their innate craving for touch, highlighting the primal nature of seeking physical connection.

We are designed to find pleasure in physical touch, sexual activities, and orgasms. It's essential to recognize that this response is a normal physiological reaction, even if we associate pleasure with past trauma or abuse. Acknowledging and accepting these sensations as natural can be a significant step towards healing from shame and self-blame associated with past traumatic events. I know, easier said than done is a massive understatement.

I feel immense anger. I'm frustrated with my father for failing to protect me, and I hold resentment toward my mother for being the one who inflicted pain upon me. It angers me that no one is aware of this situation, while my family insists that I should love her—the very person who has harmed me. I am infuriated by the fact that I found some enjoyment in it. My anger also

stems from the realization that my worth seems to be defined solely by sexual experiences. The truth is, I genuinely liked it. Now, I recognize that I was manipulated and misled; it's a significant deception. I was fooled into thinking it was acceptable because it felt good, especially considering my mother was involved. Throughout my life, I've thought that having these feelings makes me a nasty individual, but now I see it as an elaborate falsehood.

Noticing a pleasure response in the context of sexual assault will be a complex layer to your work. I promise it is doable. The job entails reconciling your confusion of experiencing pleasure and feeling dirty at the same time. Just like I'm explaining this to you now, I also needed to understand how our bodies naturally respond to touch. This piece of work is convoluted because of how incredibly baffling it is when this touch happens at an age where we can't grasp its sexual nature or reconcile the positive sensations with being abused simultaneously. We're too young to comprehend that someone who is supposed to care for us is causing harm that will take years to heal from.

I was just a little boy, but that's all I knew. As I got a little older, my mom would need my "comfort" less, but sometimes I wanted to comfort her. I could not help but shame my child self for wanting this. Now, I understand it's all I ever knew, and it felt good and normal. If my mom had given me crack cocaine, I would be addicted to that. I would have wanted it, thinking she was safe and would never do anything so horrible to harm me. I get it now and can understand why my body liked it and why I thought it was so typical.

Let's start with exercises that enhance your ability to self-soothe when you are feeling shame about how your body has responded to past sexual trauma.

EXERCISES

1. **Deep Breathing Exercises:** As you inhale and exhale slowly through your mouth, focus on the breath and try to slow down your heart rate and calm your mind. Holding a comforting object, such as a blanket or stuffed animal, can be soothing and supportive while you focus on breathing and self-care.

2. **Try Progressive Muscle Relaxation:** I like to do this lying down, but you can also do it seated. Tense and relax each muscle group in your body, starting from your toes and feet and working your way up to your head. This technique releases tension and supports a state of relaxation.

3. **Grounding Techniques:** You can feel grounded and in the present moment by lighting up all five senses. What do you see, hear, smell, touch, and taste? Your senses are so helpful in bringing you to the present moment instead of feeling overwhelmed by intrusive or shameful thoughts.

4. **Mindfulness Meditation:** Focus on what you are thinking and feeling without judgment. I prefer guided meditations that assist me in staying focused. When I get distracted, I simply return to my breath and the words spoken through the guide. Meditation is terrific in helping you become more aware of your thoughts, feelings, and body sensations without becoming overwhelmed by them.

5. **Guided Imagery:** Imagine yourself in your peaceful, safe place. Connect to all your senses and what being in this special place is like. Similar to mindful meditation, this helps calm the mind and reduce anxiety.

Remember, not all self-soothing methods will work for everyone, so finding what works best is crucial. Different techniques may work or not work on other days, so be kind to yourself, experiment with them, and be open to adjusting how you utilize them for self-care. These self-soothing tools are key in getting yourself set to tackle the particular shame linked to your body's reactions from what you experienced when you feel ready.

AFFIRMATIONS

Let the following affirmations comfort you. You are right where you need to be: learning, growing, and healing.

My body is normal for responding to pleasure.

I can learn to forgive myself and release the shame for feeling pleasure in a traumatic situation.

I can learn to trust my body as I continue to heal.

HOW DO I FEEL GOOD IN MY BODY AGAIN?

Trauma is about change you don't choose. Healing is about change you do choose.

— MICHELE ROSENTHAL

How will I feel good in my body? The next day, I remember feeling like no shower could wash him off of me. I remember scrubbing as hard as I could, but I was left feeling dirty and gross. One day, after time had passed, I finally felt clean.

So, how can you reconnect your mind and body, learn to listen to and trust your body, and finally, find a place of comfort and safety within your skin?

Part of recovering from a sexual assault and finding comfort in your body involves understanding your body's limits and forming a connection with it. Self-awareness about your body and its sensations is crucial for creating safety, setting boundaries, and feeling secure and in control of your body.

To feel good in your body, you must tune in to how your body communicates with you. This awareness enables you to feel secure and content within yourself. Often, trauma, societal norms, and family upbringing influence us to disconnect our minds from our bodies from an early age. This disconnect can manifest in various ways, such as unhealthy relationships with food, feeling pressured to finish everything on your plate regardless of fullness, or conforming to unrealistic beauty standards through dieting and exercise. Or, when having a gut feeling not to go somewhere or spend time with someone, we, as women especially, have learned to negate the gut (also known as women's intuition) and rationalize in our minds why proceeding is the best choice.

I cannot tell you how often I have ignored my gut instincts, only to find myself in extraordinarily uncomfortable or distressing situations. It doesn't always have to manifest in the context of something as severe as a sexual assault; sometimes, the consequences are subtler yet still significant. For example, there have been times when I neglected my need for self-care, convincing myself that I could push through fatigue or stress to prioritize others or fulfill external obligations.

Ignoring my own needs leads to feelings of resentment or burnout, which only compounds the discomfort. Whether it's neglecting to take a break when you're overwhelmed or disregarding your intuition about a social situation that doesn't feel right, each instance reinforces the idea that our instincts are there to protect us. It's a reminder that tuning into and honoring our feelings is a luxury and a necessity for our well-being.

Reclaiming comfort in your body post-assault is undeniably challenging due to the pressure to move on and potential feelings of betrayal by your own body. It's tricky navigating through these layers of detachment between mind and body while dealing with the aftermath of assault experiences that may have left you feeling disillusioned or disgusted with your physical self.

Feeling creepy, ugly, untouchable, unworthy, and unlovable? I've been there too. As we chatted about earlier, getting back to feeling good in your skin starts with showing yourself some love and care. Your body? It deserves compassion, gentleness, and so much tenderness. It does not deserve to be mistreated or punished in any way. You've already been through enough, so prioritizing self-love and self-care over self-punishment is crucial.

One of the best ways I learned to reconnect to feeling safe in my body post-assault was through the practice of yoga, specifically trauma-informed yoga. Yoga is a gentler way to ease into feeling at home in your body again. You can engage in yoga alone or alongside other therapies like EMDR or somatic therapy (both treatments will be explained later). Yoga is excellent for trauma survivors because it works to heal the mind, body, and spirit.

Here's how trauma-informed yoga can specifically help you:

Trauma-informed yoga is a specialized way of practicing yoga that considers how trauma affects both the body and mind. The main aim is to establish a secure and encouraging setting for people who have been through traumatic events like sexual assault.

Teachers trained in trauma-informed yoga are well-versed in the impact of trauma on the nervous system and its physical manifestations. They focus on ensuring participants feel safe, empowered, and in control, allowing them to engage in yoga at their own pace for comfort and healing.

Trauma-informed yoga involves creating a welcoming environment, providing pose variations, highlighting mindfulness practices, and avoiding anything that might trigger adverse reactions. The ultimate goal is to aid you in developing resilience, regulating your nervous system (which is so helpful when managing triggers), and re-establishing a positive connection with your body.

Another powerful way I learned to connect to my body and feel safe was through breathwork. Aside from EMDR therapy, this was some of the most powerful and emotionally releasing work I have ever done! In my experience with breathwork, I experienced a profound shedding of deep-seated shame and pain that resonated at my core. It was an intense yet remarkable sensation of liberation as I processed repressed memories and emotions that had been holding me back ever since childhood.

Breathwork can benefit you in a few ways:

1. **Getting Grounded and Focused:** Using breathwork techniques helps survivors stay present and focus on their breathing, which is helpful when feeling anxious or overwhelmed. It's a way for survivors to connect with their bodies and manage their emotions.
2. **Handling Emotions:** Deep breathing techniques are great for managing feelings of stress, anxiety, or fear that might come up because of the assault memories. By concentrating on their breath, survivors can bring calm and relaxation to their bodies, which is key for emotional healing.
3. **Letting Go of Trauma:** Breathwork aids in releasing stored trauma and tension in the body. Through specific breathing exercises, survivors can access and let go of emotions and memories that have been locked within since the assault.
4. **Feeling Empowered and Connected:** Breathwork helps survivors feel empowered and more connected to themselves. By focusing on their breath and being self-aware, survivors can gain control over their healing journey. This is crucial for regaining autonomy and self-care after experiencing trauma.

Remember, while breathwork is helpful, it's just one piece of the puzzle regarding feeling safe and comfortable in your body. There are different types of breathwork classes and guides, so researching and finding the right fit takes time. Look online or ask your therapist for a referral. Check out reviews, explore online or in-person options, and ultimately follow your gut when picking the right class or guide for this part of your healing.

Starting gently and being attuned to what feels right for yourself is essential when beginning the journey toward reconnecting with your body and cultivating compassion. The types of practices listed above serve as an excellent avenue for gentle care, self-love, and enhancing awareness of bodily sensations. By becoming comfortable in your body through these practices, you can rediscover the freedom and comfort necessary for intimacy.

Last but not least, mindful meditation has dramatically impacted my healing journey. It enabled me to manage my emotions more effectively and reduce my reactivity in certain situations. I began with short sessions of 5 minutes of guided meditation a few days each week. Now, I engage in daily practices that include longer guided sessions and utilize my meditation app to help me relax as I drift off to sleep. Through meditation, I have learned to reconnect my mind with my body, become aware of bodily sensations, and approach them with curiosity rather than judgment. This practice was an excellent introduction to trusting my body and understanding its signals.

Moreover, mindful meditation taught me how to connect with my inner child. I learned to acknowledge her presence, listen to her needs, and show her love. Although I knew her better than anyone else, she often felt unheard, isolated, and worthless. Guided meditations helped me rebuild a safe relationship with her, allowing me to understand how to nurture her when I recognized her needs.

Mindful Meditation can benefit you in the following ways:

1. **Increased Body Awareness:** Mindful meditation encourages you to concentrate on physical sensations, cultivating a deeper awareness of your body. This heightened awareness can facilitate a better understanding of how various emotions and thoughts are physically expressed.
2. **Reduced Anxiety and Stress:** Consistent practice of mindfulness can diminish anxiety and stress levels, which often contribute to discomfort in your body. Observing thoughts and feelings without judgment can nurture a sense of calm and acceptance.
3. **Enhanced Self-Acceptance:** Mindfulness promotes self-acceptance and compassion. Through non-judgmental awareness (sometimes challenging for you perfectionists), you

can learn to appreciate your body the way it is, which can reduce negative self-talk and improve body image.

4. **Improved Focus and Concentration:** Mindful meditation can boost concentration and focus, making you more attuned to your bodily sensations and emotions. This increased awareness can lead to a deeper connection with your body and an increased ability to honor your body's needs.

5. **Emotional Regulation:** Mindfulness practices help you recognize and manage emotional responses. Understanding the relationship between emotions and physical sensations allows you to navigate discomfort with greater ease and resilience.

6. **Promotion of Relaxation:** Mindful meditation encourages relaxation, alleviating muscle tension and physical discomfort. This relaxation response can help you feel more at ease in your body.

7. **Mind-Body Connection:** Practicing mindfulness strengthens the connection between the mind and body. This interconnectedness allows you to value and honor your body for its capabilities rather than concentrating solely on appearance.

8. **Encouragement of Healthy Habits:** Mindfulness can lead to more intentional decisions regarding nutrition, exercise, and self-care, enhancing overall well-being and comfort in your body.

9. **Cultivation of Gratitude:** Mindful meditation can nurture a sense of gratitude for your body, highlighting your strengths and abilities instead of fixating on perceived imperfections.

These resources are essential and fundamental for achieving a sense of well-being in your body, potentially for the first time. After collaborating with a unique client who struggled with feelings of disconnection and insecurity in her skin, she engaged in the practices I outlined here, as well as EMDR therapy. As a result, she discovered an entirely new approach to feeling connected and secure within herself. Her healing journey reached a beautiful resolution, and this is what she expressed:

Carrying Emptiness Can Feel So Heavy

I have felt disconnected for so long. I am disconnected from my authenticity, from honest, authentic relationships, from my feelings, from my reality, from my body, and my "self."

I felt alone, even in a room full of people. I held my mask up of whatever face I thought they wanted me to reflect to them. I attached their feelings to myself because I didn't know which one to pick to please them—always wanting to please. Always silently begging for their attention and love.

My body carried so many memories that had been imprinted upon it. The sadness and shame. The secrets and lies. I didn't know how to carry that attention and love I longed for. Carrying emptiness can feel so heavy.

So, I made up my mind, decided to heal, and slowly opened up to who I was meant to be.

Now, I fully live inside my body. The body that I had disassociated with for so long. The body that I used and abused. The body I used to feel pleasure, but not joy. The body I degraded and called names... fat, ugly, lazy, too big, too jiggly, too... too much.

But today, to hold, honor, and be grateful for this body fills me. Each stretch mark... every scar... all my wrinkles and crevices prove that I have lived, really lived, loved, and loved well.

This body that gave life to my boys. This body that embraces and comforts a friend. This body was strong enough to withstand abuse, neglect, and abandonment. This body that holds my heart is full of love for my family..., fellow humans... God... and myself... finally for myself.

I now connect authentically, in beautiful relationships... to my emotions... to my "self," and hold that sacred.

EXERCISE

Please consider a simple way to begin connecting with your body this week. Can you engage in deep breathing exercises? I suggest attending a dance or yoga session. Select one activity from the options provided and observe how it impacts you. Experiment with various methods of body connection, taking your time, practicing patience, and ultimately being gentle with yourself as your body seeks comfort and security. Use your journal to write down what you notice regarding thoughts, feelings, and body sensations. Doing so will help integrate what you're learning and how you are connecting to your body.

AFFIRMATIONS

The following affirmations facilitate a reframing of how you view your body. You are developing a new trust and understanding that will empower you to move forward!

I am a survivor. My body is a survivor.

I can learn to see my body as a safe place for me.

My body can be trusted to communicate to me what it needs.

Chapter Six

HOW DO I GET PAST MY AVERSION TO INTIMACY?

Healing doesn't mean the damage never existed. It means the damage no longer controls our lives.

— AKSHAY DUBEY

After multiple sexual traumas throughout my life, I find myself constantly thinking about the events and how gross and damaged I feel. I used to be fine, but I just can't get the images and disgusting feelings to go away. I have no desire for intimacy with my husband, and I feel horrible. I'm failing him and our marriage. I love him, but his touch makes me feel dirty. Sex is painful, both emotionally and physically, and I have no idea how to make this better. I think my husband will eventually leave me, and I'm terrified.

As a survivor of rape or sexual assault, one common challenge you might be dealing with is how to overcome feelings of guilt, especially if intimacy now feels uncomfortable. Sometimes, this discomfort happens right after a sexual assault, and sometimes, it does not develop until later in life, depending on your personal experience. It can be puzzling, correct? You used to be okay with intimacy, but after the assault, maybe you buried those feelings so deeply that being free and enjoying intimacy was no big deal.

Some clients have inquired about the sudden onset of painful sex or the triggering of memories and nightmares related to past assaults after years of feeling "fine." They are confused, ashamed, and fearful and struggle with knowing how to navigate this, especially within the context of an intimate relationship. In addition, partners of sexual assault survivors are equally as confused, adding to the challenge of being able to feel safe and comfortable with intimacy. Let me explain what is happening with your aversion to intimacy and what you're going to be able to do about it.

Your body may not have immediately responded to the aftermath of the assault through symptoms like nightmares, anxiety, panic, tearfulness, and hypervigilance. However, it is not unusual for the trauma to be suppressed initially, only to resurface later when your body feels secure enough to confront and process it. If this resonates more with your experience, you may perceive these occurrences as abnormal or struggle with sexual intimacy unexpectedly. When my clients experience this, I encourage them with a new mindset. For example, instead of making you feel broken, try viewing this as an opportunity for trauma processing instead. This new mindset can help you reframe these challenges as signals that your body is ready for healing. It's an opportunity for you to be free!

After a sexual assault, intimacy may or may not be painful – not because there's anything physically wrong with you; your body is intact and healthy. It's more about feeling unsafe in close connections or with touch. Your body might tense up, hindering natural responses like lubrication or hormonal functions that make sex pleasurable. It's also common to have flashbacks during intimate moments despite being with a caring partner in a safe setting, making intimacy frightening and undesirable.

These reactions are all normal when it comes to post-assault experiences with intimacy. The shift from comfort to avoidance is typical and nothing to feel ashamed about.

Childhood sexual trauma often leads survivors to perceive all physical contact as wrong or repulsive. Perhaps you have internalized this message yourself. As you embark on your healing journey, it's essential to engage in a process of relearning, allowing you to recognize that being sexually touched as a child was neither acceptable nor consensual. However, as an adult, you can embrace touch as enjoyable and exciting.

If you are a survivor of childhood sexual assault, maybe you have avoided intimacy altogether. Feeling a sexual connection with someone can trigger immediate feelings of disgust, shame, and grossness. You may feel the need to isolate for fear of developing any attraction that can lead to a flirtation, which could quickly spiral into guilt and shame. Reconciling the conflicting emotions of what happened to you as a child and how to engage in intimacy as an adult is doable, as you deserve to feel sexual pleasure.

Whether you are a survivor of childhood sexual trauma or experienced it as an adult, someone has violated your boundaries, and your body has endured significant trauma. The aversion to intimacy is a normal trauma response, and learning how to be present and create safety is of utmost importance.

This process allows you to show yourself kindness and understanding for the challenges you have encountered. The upcoming exercises will support your progress, guiding you towards re-establishing intimacy while prioritizing your safety.

Prioritizing safety is fundamental for cultivating a sense of comfort and trust within your own body. Similar to the visible healing of physical wounds, emotional healing also progresses one step at a time. Engaging in the exercises below is about creating safety for yourself within intimacy. Listen to more of this client's story after she implemented the tools below:

After learning new tools, learning how to create safety for myself, as well as EMDR therapy, I find myself replaying past events less and less. I started terrified that I would never be able to be intimate again and that my husband would inevitably leave me. I have worked to compartmentalize the feelings stirred up by my trauma and have chosen to focus on my love for my husband. He's my most ardent supporter, and I know sexual intimacy is vital to him, as it is to me. Once we get started, 99 times out of 100, I'm thrilled with my choice. I also know I can put on the brakes at any point and stop. We have explicitly discussed my boundaries, which he has embraced.

EXERCISES

1. Consider what makes you comfortable and secure in intimate situations. Do you prefer lights on or off? Keeping clothes on or going bare? Are there specific touches that bring up past experiences? Identify which parts of your body are okay to be touched. It's OK to take things slow and allow your body to rediscover positive sensations when touched affectionately by a trusted partner.

2. Create a safe place. Remember your sacred haven from the introduction? You can go to this place in your mind's eye before engaging in intimacy. Imagine a cozy and secure spot just like you would in guided imagery. It could be a comfy room, a hammock on the beach, a trail in nature, or even a land far away protected by giants or fire-breathing dragons! Engage all your senses to immerse yourself in this haven fully. Take every little detail of its appearance, listen to the sounds around you, and feel its ambiance. Imagine what you hear, smell, taste, and touch. Connecting to all your senses strengthens the ability to feel the importance of being present in your safe space. Spend some time in this comforting place and visit it whenever you need to relax and find peace within yourself.

3. Imagine your mindful container to lock away past baggage or distractions, allowing you to be present and embrace intimacy fully. This container can be as big as you need – think bank vault, prison cell, storage unit, shipping container, or even a deep-sea submarine! The key is to secure away anything that pulls you away from the now, whether it's old wounds or work stress. You hold the key to this lock-up; take charge and stay in the moment. Once done, retreat to your safe space, unwind, and revel in being truly present. These tricks help ground you in yourself and enhance moments of closeness.

4. Another helpful tip is to visualize yourself with your partner, picturing how it would feel to be relaxed, experience pleasure, and engage in physical intimacy without any worries. By practicing these scenarios in your mind, your body can gradually ease into it, preparing you for real-life moments of intimacy.

AFFIRMATIONS

(I am learning) I have nothing to feel guilty or ashamed about.

(I am learning) It can be safe to let others close.

(I am learning) My body is not broken.

(I am learning) I can feel safe in my body again.

Chapter Seven

HOW DO I LEARN TO SET BOUNDARIES AND SAY NO?

We need to take responsibility for claiming our hearts as our property and working on our weaknesses so that we can better respond to love.

— (CLOUD & TOWNSEND, 2007)

Before Melissa learned how to have boundaries, she shared this story.

Despite my lack of enthusiasm, my boyfriend requested a kiss and some time together. Although I had my doubts, I hesitantly complied. However, the interaction soon escalated to a more intimate level, causing me to feel progressively uneasy. Later, I confided in Lesley that I never rejected his advances because I was afraid of how he would react, especially since he had previously responded poorly when I attempted to establish boundaries or when I tried to end the relationship; he would use self-harm as a means of manipulation. It worked every time because I was terrified he would hurt himself.

In every relationship, having boundaries is crucial. Why? Because they create the best sense of safety. The strength of these boundaries varies based on how safe and secure the relationship feels. For many who have survived sexual assault, figuring out when and where to set boundaries can be one of the hardest things to do. It's natural to feel scared about setting boundaries, as doing so might upset others, just as Melissa expressed. She feared making her boyfriend feel rejected or you may worry about offending someone with your opinions. That's why this book has a section dedicated to emphasizing the significance of boundaries. I want you to understand that speaking up and setting boundaries is vital for your sense of relationship safety. Please know this: setting boundaries doesn't make you mean; it shows that you respect yourself enough to define what's acceptable for your well-being in mind, body, and spirit.

On my healing journey, a significant breakthrough occurred when I learned to establish boundaries by gaining confidence in my voice. Interestingly, while I could assert boundaries in my professional life, I consistently silenced my voice in my personal life, doubting its significance. Having experienced my first assault at a young age, I internalized the belief that my body was merely a vessel for others' gratification. It wasn't until I had gone through two marriages and was searching for a meaningful connection that I came to understand the importance of my voice and realized I no longer needed to rely on my body to feel loved.

Through therapy, self-reflection, confronting the events that had made me feel worthless, and all the exercises I teach you in this book, I began to recognize my inherent value, even if I didn't initially feel it. This process ultimately enabled me to cultivate confidence in my voice and establish boundaries that ensured my safety and the well-being of my body.

So, let's break down why setting boundaries in relationships is super important.

1. **Respect Is Key:** Boundaries help us show respect for each

other by clearly defining what's acceptable and what's not. It's all about caring for each other's feelings and needs.

2. **Protect Your Feelings:** You're looking out for your emotional well-being by setting boundaries. It's like creating a shield to eliminate negativity that could ruin your happiness.

3. **Keep the Conversations Flowing:** Boundaries make communication easier and more honest. When you lay down your boundaries, there's less chance of misunderstandings and arguments.

4. **Take Care of You:** Boundaries give you the space to focus on yourself and what you need. It's like hitting pause to avoid getting too overwhelmed and keep the balance between your personal life and your relationships.

5. **Healthy Vibes Only:** Boundaries build a strong foundation of trust, understanding, and compromise in a relationship. You feel safe and secure, knowing you respect each other's needs.

6. **Keeps Toxicity at a Distance:** Establishing healthy and secure relationships is the primary objective, aiming to maintain a safe distance from individuals who exhibit toxicity, lack safety, or disrespect. By doing so, you can effectively diminish triggering trauma responses when engaging with others.

So, boundaries are the secret sauce to keeping your relationships safe and healthy which is key throughout your healing process. Boundaries help with respect, communication, emotional well-being, and self-care. Boundaries are NOT about telling others (or when others tell you) to act differently or change who they (or you) are. Boundaries ARE about communicating that if others choose to treat you a certain way, i.e., yell at you, you will also act in a certain way, i.e., exit the situation until voices can be calm.

So that you know, those who genuinely care about you will always respect your limits. You shouldn't have to struggle to make others acknowledge and honor your boundaries. When I finally experienced this in my life, it was shocking! For the first time, I encountered an individual who regarded my physical being and personal boundaries with genuine respect. He wanted to understand me better, nurture a true friendship, and allow the physical elements to evolve naturally, built on trust. As our relationship advanced, he consistently sought my consent —not just at the beginning but throughout our interactions. This new way of connecting was genuinely astonishing to me! He demonstrated and illustrated that such a man could exist. He recognized my worth beyond my physical appearance. In psychological terms, we refer to this as a "corrective experience." I had finally discovered my match and never felt more comfortable, secure, appreciated, and liberated!

How individuals react to your boundaries can give you a clear picture of who you can trust. You may need to set firmer boundaries with those who aren't safe but with whom you still want to connect. With trustworthy ones, you can have more flexible boundaries that allow for closer interactions and intimacy.

I teach my clients to think of boundaries like this: Many homes have fences around them to mark their space. Imagine if your neighbor dumped their garbage on your lawn—if you tend to please others, you might just clean it up without question. However, this inevitably will lead to complaining and resentment on your part. But wait, why should their mess become your problem? Someone with healthy boundaries would assertively tell them to take care of their trash.

Just as physical boundaries protect property, we need emotional, financial, relational, and spiritual boundaries for ourselves. This way, we can distinguish what burdens (trash) we carry from those that do not belong to us.

Do you struggle with carrying other people's trash? If so, this behavior often originates from early conditioning to ensure others are happy at your own expense. This people-pleasing ultimately teaches you to place a higher value on others' well-being at your sacrifice. Previous attempts at setting boundaries may have been met with accusations of selfishness, guilt, shame, or manipulation (as in Melissa's case), further reinforcing the pattern of neglecting your own needs.

As you may have experienced, carrying others' trash at your expense is unsustainable for your emotional well-being. The lack of clearly defined or respected boundaries can lead to resentment, frustration, and anger, as you may feel taken advantage of, disrespected, or overwhelmed when your personal space, time, or emotions are invaded or disregarded. And just so you know, resentment is a cancer to your soul!

Learning to say "no" without guilt or shame is incredibly freeing. I know, you're probably thinking that is impossible to fathom. But with this chapter and practice, you can get there!

EXERCISES

Setting boundaries with unhealthy or toxic people can be challenging, especially if those people are family. I always tell my clients that family is not a right but a privilege. Therefore, if your family is toxic, you still need to do what you can to have a voice and create your safety. Here are some things to think about and start to practice to set boundaries in your life.

These prompts will help you reflect on the factors that influence your comfort level in various situations and identify what is necessary to feel respected and valued. Start by breaking down your relationships between family, friends, co-workers, and significant others. Once you thoroughly understand your boundaries, focus on effectively communicating them to others.

1. **Identify Toxic Behaviors:** It is time to take out your journal and get specific regarding the behaviors or actions that cause you to feel unsafe or uncomfortable. For example, do I feel valued and respected in my relationship with mom, dad, siblings, and extended family members? Do friends and family members (list their names) hear my voice (list them separately)? Can I be myself without judgment or critical feedback? When my friends (specific names) or family (specific members) have an issue with me, do they approach me with kindness or criticism and shame?

2. **Communicate Assertively:** This is the hard part for people pleasers. Being direct does not mean you're a bitch! Remember, boundaries are not about changing other people; they are about letting others know how you will respond if certain behaviors happen. The goal is to communicate calmly and assertively. Be specific about what behaviors are not ok and what you will do if you experience them. For example, If you yell at me, I will leave the room until you can talk calmly.

3. **Stick To Your Boundaries:** This is harder than you think. Once you have set the boundaries, you might get pushback. If so, stay calm and consistent. Tolerance of violations teaches the other person that you're either not serious about the boundaries or don't believe they are essential.

4. **Limit Your Time:** Limit your time interacting with toxic people. This boundary may mean avoiding or setting time limits in certain situations. For example, instead of visiting family for 2 weeks, how about 3 days? Or, instead of staying through that whole party, drop by, say hello, and bow out.

5. **Practice Self-Care:** Taking time and care for yourself is ESSENTIAL when dealing with toxic people. Make time for activities that bring you peace, joy, safety, fun, and relaxation to help maintain your overall well-being.

6. **Seek Support:** If boundaries feel overwhelming or too scary, consider getting with a therapist and learning to assert your voice and express your boundaries.

Engaging in role-playing scenarios can be a beneficial method for practicing boundary setting. Enlist the support of a trusted friend or family member to act as someone who challenges your boundaries, allowing you to practice responding assertively and respectfully. This exercise can help boost your confidence in asserting boundaries in real-life situations. If you are uncomfortable doing this, a therapist can make a great practice buddy.

7. **Learn to sit with the discomfort of upsetting others:** You can do so with deep breathing, meditation, exercise, healthy distractions, and positive self-talk that you are doing the right thing to create safety and health in your life. The goal is to remember that each individual is responsible for their emotions and reactions. Don't carry their trash!

8. **Journaling:** Journaling can be a helpful tool for exploring and tracking your journey in establishing boundaries. Document instances when you felt your boundaries were crossed, note your reactions, and reflect on alternative approaches. This practice helps you identify recurring patterns and develop strategies for establishing healthy boundaries moving forward. For example, whenever I am with so and so, I leave feeling...

Mastering the art of setting boundaries takes time and effort. Remember to be kind to yourself as you work towards establishing and upholding healthy boundaries in your relationships. Boundaries are crucial in ensuring your safety in personal connections and the world. I promise that recognizing your voice's power is a game-changer for healing!

AFFIRMATIONS

These affirmations remind and encourage you to transform how you deserve to feel in your relationships.

I deserve to be loved and treated well.

I am healing now. As I grow in love with myself and my life, I will stay away from people who don't align with that self-love.

I deserve caring relationships.

Chapter Eight

HOW DO I KNOW IF I SHOULD REPORT SEXUAL ASSAULT?

I am a survivor, not a victim. I have a voice, not just a story. I have strength, not just scars.

— UNKNOWN

I decided to report because it felt like something I could control again when I felt so out of control. I wanted to do something about what happened to me and try to keep other girls safe.

Healing from sexual assault is such a rollercoaster. It's like juggling many things simultaneously as you go through the healing journey. You could be all about finding your voice, learning to say no, kicking people pleasing to the curb, and feeling safe with physical closeness. And to add to the mix, you might also be trying to figure out whether you want to report what happened. Let's look at the pros and cons of reporting. Remember that you have the right to choose whether or not to report it.

Here are some things my client Martha had to think about when deciding whether to report her sexual assault.

1. **Safety First:** Your safety comes first. If you're in immediate danger or need medical help, prioritize your well-being.

2. **Emotional Impact:** Consider how reporting the assault might affect you emotionally. It can be tricky and challenging, so feel prepared to handle it.

3. **Support System:** Think about the people who can support you – friends, family, or a counselor who can provide emotional help during the reporting process.

4. **Legal Aspects:** If someone is charged with a crime, the state makes the accusation, and you, as the victim, serve as a witness. If the state has enough evidence to bring the case to trial and it doesn't settle out of court, you might be asked to testify.

5. **Impact on the Perpetrator:** Reporting an assault can make the perpetrator responsible for their actions and prevent them from harming others. Remember, ensuring they face consequences or never hurt anyone else is **not your job**. It's just one more thing to consider when making this tough choice.

6. **Community Support Services:** Reporting the assault could connect you with support services for counseling and healing resources. It's all about empowerment and validating your experience.

In the end, reporting sexual assault is a personal choice with no right or wrong answer. Do what feels best for you and focus on your well-being.

There are potential drawbacks to reporting sexual assault to consider when deciding whether to report it and pursue legal action.

1. **Re-traumatization:** The legal process of prosecuting sexual assault can re-traumatize survivors by making them relive details of the assault multiple times and facing the perpetrator in court. Sometimes, the questions asked to the victim can be insensitive and make it seem like you're responsible. This

situation is infuriating, and there is a clear need for improved training within law enforcement agencies.

2. **Lack of Evidence:** Proving sexual assault in court can be challenging without physical evidence like a rape kit or witnesses, leading to a lack of accountability for the perpetrator and a sense of helplessness on the part of the victim.

3. **Public Scrutiny:** Reporting sexual assault and being part of a legal case may expose survivors to public judgment and scrutiny. Deciding whether to take legal action against sexual assault can be challenging. The legal process can drag on, draining your emotions and prolonging your healing journey. Feeling unsupported or doubted by the system only adds to the stress.

After considering all of the above, my client was willing to testify. After testifying, she shared how she felt.

> *I felt powerful after testifying. I felt like I had taken my power back and stood up for myself. It's a feeling I'll never forget.*

Statistics show that the prosecution rate for sexual assault is relatively low compared to other crimes. Around 35% of assaults are reported to police, and even fewer lead to arrests and prosecutions. Keep in mind that these numbers can differ by location and case specifics.

One high-profile example of a successful prosecution is the Larry Nassar case. Nassar, a former doctor for the USA Gymnastics team and Michigan State University, was sentenced to up to 175 years in prison for numerous counts of assault and child pornography against gymnasts meant to be under his care. This case shed light on abuse, accountability, and athlete protection issues. It also emphasized how crucial it is for survivors to speak up, the role of investigative journalism, and the necessity for systemic changes to prevent future instances of sexual abuse in sports and other institutional settings.

Not every case captures public attention, nor do all result in a guilty verdict. In the above client's situation, her assailant was acquitted, which was profoundly disheartening for her. However, with the backing of myself, her family, and friends, she retained her sense of empowerment, renewed her pride for standing up for herself, and discovered avenues to advocate positively.

If the individual who sexually assaulted you is acquitted, it can be a harrowing and emotionally taxing ordeal. Here are some steps you can take to move on.

1. **Consider Other Options:** If the legal system doesn't deliver the desired result, consider alternative ways to seek justice, such as civil litigation or advocacy initiatives.
2. **Be An Advocate For Change:** Utilize your experience to push for improvements in legal procedures, policies, and societal attitudes towards sexual assault. Participate in advocacy groups or campaigns that aid survivors and combat sexual violence.

Remember that healing is a personal journey; there is no right or wrong way to navigate life after an acquittal. Be patient and kind with yourself as you progress toward regaining control over your well-being.

Here is another example illustrating how hard this decision to report or not to report can be. A young lady contacted me on social media and agreed to let me share her story. Please be aware that her story can be very triggering. Ensure your safety tools (from the introduction) are in place before reading her experience.

> *When I was around 4 years old, I started acting out because my mom had another child, and it made me feel like I wasn't getting her love and attention any more. Looking back at home videos, I can see how those emotions were already there. Fast forward to my parents' divorce, and my mom quickly remarried a "good Christian" man. This stepdad took my side, noticing how my mom was mistreating me, and he tried to show me love.*

In hindsight, he groomed me, which eventually led to a sexual assault incident when I was in middle school. I bravely told my mom about it the next day.

Instead of supporting me, she accused me of trying to ruin her new marriage. It was heartbreaking, but I just apologized. My mom had a violent side, and they both put on a facade of being loving towards others and my sisters while treating me terribly behind closed doors. They even sent me to a mental institution twice and put me on birth control as a young teenager as a precaution. I cannot even tell you how stressed out I felt. Thankfully, when I turned 16, my dad gained custody of me, and things started getting better miraculously.

Recently, memories have resurfaced, making me realize the extent of the pain I endured all those years ago. Now in my 30s, with one year to report it legally in my state, I know this man works with kids, Lesley. He never admitted his wrongdoing or showed any remorse for his actions, which were deliberate and concealed. While anger is part of healing for sure, what I truly seek is closure – validation of what happened to me. Whether justice is necessary remains uncertain, but knowing he won't harm anyone else is vital as he preys on young girls, which makes me feel disgusted and utterly powerless.

Her narrative illustrates the complexity and challenges involved in making such a decision. In your situation, the struggle between choosing "the right thing" and what may be most beneficial for you represents a nuanced dilemma without a definitive correct or incorrect solution. The initial step is to practice self-compassion, recognizing that there are no absolute answers. The next step involves thoroughly examining what truly serves your interests in this situation. Finally, it's essential to understand that whatever choice you make, you have the authority to pursue what feels right for you, what fosters your sense of peace, and what equips you best for moving ahead.

EXERCISE

Write out the pros and cons of reporting and prosecuting. Check in with your body and see how each option feels. If there is a sense of peace, although very scary, then go for it. If it feels overwhelming, anxiety-producing, or like a "should," then I would caution you and remind you that it is okay not to pursue that course of action. Hashing out your feelings of ambivalence with a professional therapist can be very helpful in this process.

AFFIRMATIONS

I own my story, and no one can take that away from me.

My voice matters.

I am empowered and resilient.

Chapter Nine

HOW DO I GET THROUGH THE DAY AND FUNCTION LIKE A NORMAL PERSON?

I am not what happened to me. I am what I choose to become.

— CARL JUNG

It was our initial meeting, and she struggled to articulate her thoughts through tears. As a married woman with children, she began to recall experiences of being groomed during her teenage years. Although she was unsure why these memories were resurfacing now, they hindered her ability to function—caring for her kids, maintaining intimacy with her husband, and attending to her own needs felt impossible. She repeatedly expressed that it must be her fault. The overwhelming feelings of guilt, shame, and intrusive memories left her feeling trapped.

After some time, she expressed herself and took a deep breath. I felt a tightness in my throat and a heaviness in my chest as tears welled up in my eyes; I could empathize with her anguish, confusion, and the torment that shame can inflict. I reassured her that she was in a supportive environment where we would work together to piece everything back together. She smiled at this encouragement and shared that, for the first time, she felt a glimmer of hope for healing and returning to a sense of "normalcy." I emphasized that I would not disguise the truth—that this journey would require time—and asked for her understanding as we moved forward. I assured her I would provide essential tools aimed at helping her feel safe, grounded, and capable of loving herself again.

I often have folks, just like this client, reaching out to me, struggling with handling overwhelming emotions and doing simple self-care tasks, going to work, maintaining relationships, and just living life "normally." Dealing with sexual trauma, especially if it happened multiple times, can make you feel like your mind and body are disconnected, ultimately causing you to feel "crazy". You might find yourself just going through the motions of life, detached from yourself, and feeling like your body is not a safe place.

> *I do have little understanding of what it truly means to be "normal." Given that my abuse began early in my life and I've had to navigate a chaotic home environment, how can I even recognize what "normal" is? I'm here with you, Lesley, to reshape the false narratives and establish a new sense of "normal," whatever that may entail. To be frank, I desire this new normal to embrace vulnerability and foster self-trust so that I can acknowledge my intrinsic worth rather than rely on external validation and stop tying my value to my physical appearance.*

As with this client, I want to help you explore ways to redefine what normal means for you, accept your version of normal, embrace new tools to cope, and find the strength to progress with confidence and self-worth.

It can be tricky and disheartening when your emotions are so overpowering that you don't know how to cope. That feeling of being overwhelmed usually means you're "triggered," meaning your emotions are flooding your ability to function in a way that feels normal.

Curious about triggers? In the realm of post-traumatic stress disorder (PTSD), a trigger is something that sets off intense emotional or physical reactions in people who have been through trauma. Triggers vary from person to person – they could be sights, sounds, smells, places, people, or situations that remind you of the traumatic event. When triggered, those with PTSD may feel extreme fear, anxiety, distress, and panic, along with physical symptoms like a racing heart, tight chest, or sweating. Healing involves recognizing triggers and finding ways to handle them, which we will do by the end of this chapter.

After experiencing an assault from behind during a walk in the park, I found it incredibly difficult to handle anyone approaching me from that direction without a strong reaction. My son, unaware of the effect his actions had on me, would sometimes quietly enter my room after having a nightmare and stand silently by my bed, waiting for me to awaken. When I opened my eyes and saw him there, a wave of anxiety would wash over me, leaving me disoriented and terrified. Even when a loved one approached me from behind, my instinct was to jump; although I knew they meant no harm, the fear of facing danger kept me in a heightened state of alertness.

Triggers alert the brain to potential threats, regardless of whether they are real or merely perceived. The brain's primary function is to ensure survival. A trigger activates the nervous system, prompting responses such as fight, flight, freeze, or fawn (submission or people-pleasing). I often despised my intense reactions to these triggers and frequently felt irrational or crazy. To manage the profound emotional distress I encountered, I looked for coping strategies, often not the healthiest of choices.

Like so many of my clients, I turned to drugs, alcohol, and an eating disorder to numb out, avoid, and try to control my life. These were quick fixes to escape feeling uneasy or struggling to handle life when emotions got overwhelming. While it was not the best long-term solution for my overall health and well-being, I now know it is a common way for people to cope with these intense feelings and challenges.

After going through a traumatic experience, victims often find themselves feeling powerless in nearly all aspects of their lives. This loss of control can lead to feelings of fear, unease, and heightened alertness, resulting in a chaotic nervous system. Like myself, some may turn to substances as a means to dull these feelings, which can create an illusion of regaining control. The body instinctively seeks ways to restore a sense of control, whether through healthy or unhealthy methods. Consequently, survivors of sexual assault frequently exhibit substance abuse and eating disorders.

According to the National Eating Disorders Association (NEDA), research suggests that up to 30% of individuals with eating disorders have experienced some form of sexual trauma, including sexual assault. It's important to note that this statistic may vary depending on different studies and populations.

The emergence of an eating disorder can often be an unconscious effort to reclaim a sense of authority over one's life, just like it was for me. Reflecting on my journey, I wish I had recognized this truth during my formative years when I faced immense struggles with body image and food restrictions. In chapter 3, I recounted my experience as a small child with a family friend whom I trusted, who visited our home when I was too ill to go to preschool. It wasn't until much later that memories surfaced—vague yet haunting—of an inappropriate examination that left me feeling profoundly uncomfortable in his presence after that. Although those memories remain shrouded in fog, I understand that my body holds wisdom about that experience, reminding me of the crossed boundaries and the feelings of being unclean and out of control that followed.

Whether restricting, binging, purging, exercising excessively, or obsessively controlling what you eat, these behaviors restore a feeling of power over your life.

Not all coping mechanisms may seem logical or rational. In addition to substances and my eating disorder, I also turned to promiscuity in a subconscious attempt to try and reconcile jurisdiction, safety, and connection. It may seem counterintuitive to turn to sex as a way to cope. Nevertheless, it is common, especially if your sexual assault happened at a young age. Like me, you discovered that you could use your body to seek connection, attention, validation, or even a sense of love. Despite the temporary relief it may bring, it sadly often leads to feelings of shame, intense loneliness, and self-blame afterward.

Here is an example of a client whose primary means of escape was pornography. Despite the immense shame it caused him, he seemed to recognize no alternative vices for alleviating his suffering. He had come to believe that sexual experiences were the sole source of his sense of value and self-worth.

> *I am always afraid, stressed out, and scared. I know my mom's sexual abuse and my dad's physical abuse are not my fault; however, I always hear my parents' voices in my head telling me I'm not good enough, I'm bad, and everything that makes me myself is terrible. I don't know who I am, so I have to hide parts of myself which always leads me to porn. I feel so ashamed and responsible.*

Have you found yourself dealing with unhealthy coping mechanisms in your day-to-day life? Maybe you've noticed that you're stuck in a cycle of using substances, struggling with eating habits, pornography, or other behaviors that aren't giving you a sense of life and empowerment. Sometimes, just realizing that these actions are an attempt at coping can come as a surprise. It can be a lightbulb moment that helps you break free from those habits and look for healthier ways to handle your triggers.

It all begins with two key ideas. First is establishing a fresh "normal." Then, you've got to permit yourself to mourn what used to be and who you were before the assault. These two things go hand in hand. For instance, reflect on your pre-assault self. Let yourself experience the sorrow of losing your innocence, your feeling of freedom, and security. Allowing these emotions and grieving the past creates room to shape your present self. Remember, you're not accountable for what occurred, but you hold the power to navigate through it and recover. Now, deciding who you want to become is up to you.

Here is what not to do when creating your new normal and idea of who you get to be:

1. Don't compare yourself to your past self.
2. Don't compare to other sexual assault survivors.
3. Don't compare to anyone else – ever!

When you compare yourself to your former self or others, things spiral downward. I call it the "shame" spiral. You will never feel good enough or adequate when comparing. You have heard that comparison is the thief of joy, and nothing could be more accurate.

Here is what you can do instead:

1. Picture a day when you feel on top of the world. Don't dwell on who you used to be; focus on what you dream of experiencing when feeling like a queen or king.
2. Imagine waking up refreshed, meditating, breaking a sweat, having a nutritious breakfast, crushing it at work, hanging out with besties later, and then drifting off into a peaceful slumber, feeling secure.
3. Envision practicing healthy self-care, setting good boundaries, and having energy and joy in your day.

These are just a few ways to envision and kickstart your vision of your fresh normal. Sure, past trauma might set some barriers for now, but remember that it's all about baby steps as you heal. Everyone has their limits to work with. As these barriers shift and change over time depending on where you're at, your idea of normal will adapt, too.

Instead of resorting to harmful coping mechanisms, there are healthier alternatives that can help you manage intense emotions, connect to your genuine self, and feel safe in your own body. As humans, it is hard to take something away without replacing it with something else. As you consider letting go of what no longer serves you, I will suggest replacements to try.

There are several practical tools for regulating emotions, navigating triggers, and learning how to feel safe in your skin while starting to create your new normal. Here are some techniques that can help:

1. **Mindfulness and Meditation:** Mindfulness and meditation can help you become more aware of your emotions as you learn to observe them without judgment. Meditation can help you regulate your emotions more effectively. My favorite meditation app is called *Insight Timer*. Over 35,000 free guided meditations are available to help you care for your mind and body when you feel intense emotions. Developing a daily practice changes brain chemistry and calms the entire nervous system. Try it for a few minutes a day for a week and see what you notice!

2. **Deep breathing exercises**: Deep breathing exercises can help calm your nervous system, reduce feelings of stress and anxiety, and handle triggers. Here are three great breathing exercises you can try. I recommend doing deep breathing exercises daily.
   - **Deep Breathing Technique:** Find a quiet and comfortable place to sit or lie down. Close your eyes and take a deep breath through your nose, allowing your belly to expand as you fill your lungs with air. Hold your breath for a few seconds, then slowly exhale through your mouth, letting out all the air. Repeat this process for several minutes, focusing on the sensation of your breath entering and leaving your body.

- ○ **4-7-8 Breathing Technique**: This involves inhaling for a count of 4, holding your breath for a count of 7, and exhaling for a count of 8. Start by exhaling completely, then inhale quietly through your nose for a count of 4. Hold your breath for a count of 7, then exhale slowly and completely through your mouth for a count of 8. Repeat this cycle for a few minutes, allowing yourself to relax and unwind with each breath.
- ○ **Breathe Colors**: Let's try this nifty trick. Inhale a specific color, then exhale a different one. It's like a chill way to tune into your body and find your zen. For instance, take in the calming blue and release the fiery red. Or just go with whatever colors vibe with you at the moment!

3. **Physical Exercise**: Regular exercise can help regulate your emotions by releasing endorphins, natural mood boosters. Even a short walk or quick workout can help improve your mood. If you're not a regular exerciser, try starting slow with a 5–10-minute walk daily. Try it for a week and see how it makes you feel.

4. **Journaling:** Writing down your thoughts and feelings can help you process and make sense of your emotions. Try writing in a journal about your experiences and how they make you feel. Have a notepad handy at work and home so you can easily express your feelings. If you're mourning your old "normal" self, you can write yourself a goodbye letter and then write your new self a welcome letter. This can be a powerful exercise to try. If it feels too triggering, please take this exercise to a therapist who will support you through it.

5. **Social Support:** Talking to a friend, family member, or therapist can provide emotional support and help you process your feelings. Connecting with others can help you feel less alone in your emotions. Therapy is key in this journey. Having a safe space to express your feelings without fear of judgment can help you heal and learn how to regulate your thoughts and feelings. Feeling secure, seen, and heard is imperative for your healing journey.

6. **Self-care Activities:** Engaging in activities that you enjoy and help you relax, such as taking a bath, reading a book, or listening to music, can help regulate your emotions and improve your overall well-being. What is one small and doable thing you can do for yourself daily?

Everyone is different, so finding the best tools for you may take trial and error. Being patient and kind as you explore various emotional regulation strategies is essential. By incorporating these practices into your life, you can work towards feeling more balanced and at peace within yourself. These coping mechanisms are excellent replacements for those not truly serving you.

As you navigate daily life and strive to operate like others, we discussed the importance of accepting the journey of establishing a new normal, being gentle with your past experiences, and discovering effective methods for coping with triggers. These are significant forms of self-care, a valuable gift you give to yourself as you begin the journey of healing. Rather than ignoring or avoiding deep wounds from past sexual assault experiences, choose to treat yourself with kindness and empathy. By learning to handle triggers and developing a positive, empowering perspective on your life, you set out on a transformative path toward finding your new normal.

EXERCISE

Remember, offering a replacement is vital before removing an unhealthy coping mechanism. While unhealthy coping is one choice, we now have more tools and alternatives available. Let's work on expanding your toolbox so you can experiment with different options.

What is one coping mechanism from the list above that you can start to explore and practice? Make sure you are setting small, manageable goals each day. There is no room for perfection here. Gentleness and compassion will be the key to your healing.

AFFIRMATIONS

Let's end the chapter with these compassionate affirmations. Remember, you can adjust these or make ones that resonate with you. The new neural pathways you create will combat your tendency to fall prey to shame and hopelessness. The ones listed are some of my favorites!

I can learn to practice healthy coping mechanisms.

It's ok to have a healthy sense of control.

I can slowly build new, healthy habits because I am not in danger anymore.

Chapter Ten

HOW DO I HEAL WHEN I SEE MY PERPETRATOR LIVING THEIR BEST LIFE?

The strength of a survivor is immeasurable. Your resilience is your power.

— UNKNOWN

I was on a business trip when a colleague obstructed my path, preventing me from passing. This encounter left me feeling extremely uncomfortable. He began to touch me, and at first, I felt paralyzed with fear. However, I eventually managed to navigate around him and retreat to my room without further incident. I was trembling and overwhelmed with anxiety. After returning from the trip, I reported the incident to HR. During their investigation, I chose to work from home, as I no longer felt safe in the office environment. Meanwhile, he received a promotion! Ultimately, I decided to leave what had once been my dream job while he continued to thrive. I am filled with a mix of anger and sadness.

Healing from sexual assault is a complex and challenging journey that can be further complicated when survivors face the unsettling reality of seeing their perpetrators seemingly thriving and living their best lives. The experience of encountering the person who caused so much pain and trauma can evoke a range of emotions, from rage and resentment to fear and powerlessness. Let's explore the intricate healing process in the face of such circumstances, offering insights, strategies, and support for those navigating this rugged terrain. By acknowledging and validating these feelings, you can begin to reclaim your power and find a path toward healing and recovery.

Within the healing process, it's crucial not to dwell on your perpetrator's journey and compare it to yours. Comparison truly steals away any chance of finding joy and only hinders your progress toward recovery. In my practice, I call it being slimed.

> *My rapist was made captain of the football team.*
>
> *He is a high-powered lawyer with a considerable reputation. No one would believe me.*
>
> *The teacher who groomed me was voted teacher of the year!*
>
> *My abuser is now the head pastor of a mega-church.*

Believing that justice will find its way, whether in this life or beyond, is vital. Perhaps you believe in karma; karma has a way of knowing your perpetrator's address! Trust that other cosmic forces will address what occurred and hold the responsible party accountable. Redirect your focus onto yourself – prioritize creating a sense of safety, nurturing your healing journey, and keeping your gaze fixed on your well-being rather than on someone who shouldn't carry weight or power in your life anymore.

Part of the healing process involves letting go of pain, anger, and humiliation—all those emotions need acknowledgment and processing as you work through them. What if you unexpectedly cross paths with them? What if you encounter them professionally? Therapy can help you navigate and prepare for these scenarios, dealing with past traumas while gearing up for what lies ahead.

The tips to navigate this type of specific challenge are an accumulation of everything we have touched on thus far:

1. **Recognize your emotions:** It's natural to experience the anger and frustration that you are currently going through. Rather than judging yourself, allow yourself to process these emotions fully.

2. **Explore constructive ways to express your emotions:** A journal can be an excellent medium for releasing your thoughts! Additionally, engaging in artistic activities, listening to or creating music, or confiding in a trusted friend or therapist can be beneficial. Articulating your feelings aids in processing them effectively.

3. **Reframe the narrative:** Consider altering your viewpoint. Rather than concentrating on your perpetrator's life, direct your attention inward, highlighting your personal development and recovery. Acknowledge your achievements and the favorable aspects of your life for which you are grateful.

4. **Limit your exposure:** Are you still connected with this individual on social media? Do work or family commitments require your presence around them? Reducing your interaction as much as possible in face-to-face settings may be beneficial. Additionally, consider completely blocking them on social media and cutting off any means of communication, such as calls, texts, or emails, as this could alleviate some of the difficulties you are experiencing.

5. **Be deliberate in your self-care:** Focus on engaging in activities and surrounding yourself with individuals who contribute to your happiness, tranquility, and sense of purpose. Whether through pursuing a hobby, participating in volunteer work, or enjoying the company of trusted loved ones, prioritizing positive experiences while avoiding time and energy spent on those who have caused you harm can aid in transforming your perspective.

6. **Visualize your future:** Dedicate time to picture your desired life. Establish goals and strive to achieve them. This approach allows you to focus on your journey instead of fixating on the life of your perpetrator.

EXERCISES

Remember, the objective is to convert your suffering into resilience and self-assurance. Clinging to past experiences and observing your aggressor succeed will only hinder your progress. Concentrate on creating space for yourself while prioritizing your healing and overall well-being. Ultimately, the individual responsible for your distress will face repercussions, whether in this life or the next!

Select one task each week from the provided list. As you gradually create more distance and feel a sense of empowerment, the anger you experience will diminish, allowing you to release the intense negativity holding you back.

AFFIRMATIONS

What happened does not define me.

I am allowed to do things that make me feel better. I am allowed to heal.

My trauma is valid.

It's ok to let go.

Chapter Eleven

HOW DO MY BROKEN PIECES GET MENDED?

I am not what I have done. I am what I have overcome.

— UNKNOWN

It used to take over every thought of every day. And then it took over every other thought. Eventually, I was okay and knew I would be okay. I now know I'm not broken; I'm strong.

Just as this client reveals, experiencing sexual assault can be overwhelming, leaving one with the impression that they may never fully recover. It's as if someone took a wrecking ball to your inner self and shattered it into countless fragments. Each fragment carries its pain and hurt. Feeling lost and powerless to put these pieces back together is entirely understandable. This chapter will help you start the journey of healing those broken pieces so you can look towards a brighter future, feeling complete and optimistic.

The process includes mastering three critical concepts: self-compassion, self-forgiveness, and self-love. I learned about these concepts on my recovery journey. I had no idea I was so hard on myself, so hypercritical, and needed always to be perfect. My lack of self-compassion, self-forgiveness, and self-love left me in a cesspool of shame.

I now identify as a recovered perfectionist, yet I admit I can still fall into a dark place without these mindsets. Reflecting on my past, I recall the torment I endured in my unhealthy relationship with both my body and food before I embraced and practiced these transformative mindsets. I felt an overwhelming pressure to appear flawless, to eat ideally, and to have a number on the scale that met my impossible standards. If I fell short, I perceived myself as a total failure, unworthy of love and acceptance. However, discovering how to nurture myself through the lessons I am about to share was a turning point in my healing journey.

Before we begin the activities I've prepared for you in this section, it's vital to understand why these three concepts are pivotal to your recovery.

First off, let's talk about **self-compassion.** You're someone who readily extends compassion to others, right? You acknowledge that perfection is unattainable and wouldn't expect it from others. You understand that people mess up and deserve forgiveness. You recognize that individuals in pain may cause harm due to their suffering or poor choices. Have you heard the phrase "hurt people hurt people"?

However, none of these principles apply to you. You tend to be overly critical of yourself, quickly assign blame, and hold yourself to impossibly high standards.

I can promise that healing becomes much smoother and faster when you treat yourself with the same kindness, forgiveness, and love you show to those you care about. Self-compassion, forgiveness, and self-love don't allow you to act recklessly; instead, these qualities require holding yourself accountable with the same care as you would for others.

Next up is the significance of **self-forgiveness.** If others are allowed room for growth through mistakes and imperfections, why deny yourself the same opportunity? Why should you bear the burden alone while everyone else moves on freely from their errors or harmful behaviors? The forgiveness you readily offer others is equally applicable to yourself. Without forgiving yourself, progress and healing become arduous tasks.

You may not feel proud of what necessitates your forgiveness; however, context is behind it, along with valuable lessons that can positively shape your future. What's the point of being human if we are condemned for our mistakes without any chance of redemption? Instead, embrace your humanity by learning from missteps and moving forward with newfound wisdom and understanding. Hey, doesn't the latter option sound way better?

Lastly, looking after yourself is super important for your overall mental well-being. **Self-love** shows through being kind to yourself, forgiving yourself, and caring for your mind and body daily. Do you prioritize things like sleep, eating well, and having fun? That's what self-love is all about. It's about having a say in things, setting boundaries, and making choices with your well-being in mind. These three aspects are all connected and overlap a lot.

You've probably heard you can't truly love others until you love yourself first. And honestly, that's spot on. My existence focused on proving my lovability and worth, which made me great at showing love and nurturance to others, while starving myself in the process. I used to give so much that I had nothing left in my tank. Does this ring a bell for you? Once I adopted the airplane analogy of securing my mask before assisting others, I found that I could replenish my energy, allowing me to cultivate a greater capacity for caring for those around me. When you put loving yourself first, you'll have the time, energy, kindness, and love to give to others without draining yourself or causing harm.

In the journey of healing, if you too have endured a lifetime of trauma, faced moments where you have felt shattered, feared that your brokenness might hinder the success of your marriage, or struggled with believing you deserve healing and love, then now is the time that marks putting away your sense of feeling like damaged goods. Just keep in mind it's a journey, not a sprint. Embracing self-compassion, self-forgiveness, and self-love are crucial for repairing your wounded self and sense of brokenness.

EXERCISES

You can try various exercises and activities based on how you're feeling. I suggest giving one a shot each week and seeing how it goes. Stick with the ones that resonate with you and let go of the ones that don't fit. The goal is to transition from self-criticism to recognizing your worth and embracing self-love freely.

SELF-COMPASSION

Practicing self-compassion is key to your overall mental health. It may be challenging, but you will see the endless benefits if you're open to learning and practicing it. Here are some exercises to help nurture self-compassion.

1. **Self-Compassion Meditation:** Spend a few minutes daily practicing loving-kindness or self-compassion meditation. Think positive and compassionate thoughts to yourself, like "I may be kind to myself" or "I may treat myself gently." Try the *Insight Timer* App I mentioned earlier and look up "self-compassion" meditations.

2. **Self-Compassion Journaling:** Write down your thoughts and feelings using self-compassionate language. Recognize your struggles with kindness and empathy. Be mindful of harsh or critical words you tend to use and practice using words of compassion instead.

3. **Self-Compassion Letter:** Pen a letter to yourself as if comforting a friend through tough times. Provide words of encouragement, support, and understanding. To assist in this,

imagine your friend went through your trauma. What would you write to them? How would you try to encourage them or know they are hurting?

4. **Self-Care Practices:** Engage in activities that nurture your physical, emotional, and mental well-being – whether taking a relaxing bath, enjoying nature walks, practicing yoga, or simply unwinding.

5. **Boost Yourself:** Repeat positive affirmations or words of self-compassion throughout your day. Remind yourself of your value, resilience, and inner strength. I like the I Am Daily Affirmations app. It's a great way to get fresh affirmations delivered to your phone.

6. **Be Mindful of Critical Self-talk:** You may need to be aware of how critically you talk to yourself. Practice mindfulness by staying in the present moment and observing your thoughts and emotions without judgment. Treat yourself with kindness and understanding as you navigate your inner dialogue.

7. **Reach Out for Help:** Connect with supportive people, family members, or a therapist who can provide empathy, validation, and a listening ear. Opening up about your challenges can make you feel less isolated and more supported.

Just remember, self-compassion is a skill that grows with time and patience. Treat yourself kindly and extend the same care and compassion to yourself as you would to a loved one.

SELF-FORGIVENESS

Practicing forgiveness, particularly self-forgiveness, can be a significant hurdle on your healing journey. We often set unrealistically high expectations for ourselves and then feel shame when we fail to meet them. Try out these exercises to nurture a newfound ability to engage in self-forgiveness.

1. **Reflect on Your Actions:** Take a moment to ponder over any situation or mistake that's been hard for you to forgive yourself for. Consider the context, your intentions, and the lessons learned from it. Also, remember, we don't know what we don't know. Be careful not to carry blame or responsibility for situations you didn't know about.

2. **Pen an Apology Letter to Yourself:** Write down forgiveness for the wrongdoing or mistake you're holding onto. Acknowledge any guilt or shame you feel and offer yourself kindness and understanding.

3. **Show Self-Compassion:** Engage in activities like self-compassion meditation or uplifting affirmations to foster kindness and empathy toward yourself for making mistakes—even if those mistakes have serious consequences, the goal is to remember you're human.

4. **Deal with Negative Emotions:** Allow yourself to experience and work through any negative feelings that surface when reflecting on the situation. Use mindfulness techniques and prioritize self-care to handle these emotions healthily. Let yourself feel the feels. Your feelings will not kill you, I promise. Your feelings deserve to be seen, heard, honored, and finally released.

5. **Combat Self-Doubt:** Identify and challenge any critical or negative thoughts blocking your path to forgiving yourself. Swap these thoughts for more compassionate perspectives. For example, "I am too broken to heal" can be changed to "I can engage in healing and learn how to move on with my life."

6. **Lean on Your Support System:** Share your struggles with self-forgiveness with someone you trust—a friend, family member, or therapist—for valuable insights and support.

7. **Embrace Acceptance:** Accept that everyone makes mistakes. Forgiveness is a journey rather than an instant destination. Let go of guilt and shame, focusing instead on moving forward with self-compassion and personal growth. Self-forgiveness takes time and effort, so go easy on yourself as you aim to forgive and embrace your past slip-ups.

8. **Remember you are human:** As surprising as it may seem, it is essential to acknowledge your humanity. Self-forgiveness hinges on recognizing that being human entails making mistakes and harboring regrets, a universal experience we all share. Perfection is unattainable for anyone except a divine being; thus, imperfection is a natural aspect of humanity.

SELF-LOVE

The final concept that needs attention is practicing self-love. The key to going from broken to unbroken is boosting self-love. Try these tricks to nurture self-love.

1. **Pump Yourself Up:** Kickstart your day with positive affirmations like "I'm awesome," "I'm more than enough," or "I deserve love and happiness." Repeat these mantras all day long to amp up that self-love vibe. If these are hard to say out loud, add "I'm LEARNING to believe I'm awesome," "I'm LEARNING to believe I'm more than enough," etc.
2. **Me-Time Routine:** Craft a routine that pampers your body, mind, and soul. Treat yourself to a bubble bath, do some yoga, dive into a good read, or take a stroll in the great outdoors.
3. **Gratitude Log:** Keep a journal where you jot down things that made your day brighter. This habit can shift your focus to the good stuff and amp up the self-love vibes.
4. **Boundaries Rock:** Learn to say no when needed and put your well-being first by setting boundaries with others. Standing up for yourself and practicing self-care are top moves in the self-love game. Refer to chapter 7 for a deeper dive into boundaries.
5. **Zen Out:** Get into mindfulness with meditation, deep breathing, or mindful walks. Staying in the moment helps boost self-awareness and compassion towards yourself.
6. **Pat Yourself on the Back:** Celebrate your wins – big or small! Acknowledge your strengths, talents, and progress towards crushing those goals. Hug yourself!

7. **Positivity Crew:** Surround yourself with folks who lift you and engage in activities that light up your world. Creating a positive space is key for nurturing that self-love vibe.

8. **Social Media Audit:** It's essential to do a social media check-in. Be honest with yourself and unfollow or deactivate accounts that don't make you feel good or energized. You know how we said comparison is the thief of joy? Social media can easily lead to much comparing, making you feel like your life isn't measuring up. Sometimes, you might not notice how much shame creeps in after scrolling for ages. Stick to accounts that lift you, bring positivity, and make you feel valued.

9. **Mirror Talk:** While looking into a mirror, take a moment to gaze deeply into your eyes and say out loud, "I love you." I understand that this can be incredibly difficult and challenging, but it is a powerful and beautiful practice for cultivating self-love. Embracing this moment can help you connect with yourself on a deeper level and reinforce your worth. Remember, you deserve this love and affirmation!

Just remember – building self-love takes practice and patience. So be kind, understanding, and gentle as you journey towards loving and accepting yourself more deeply.

Before we conclude this chapter, I want to share some encouragement. Feeling shattered is among the most distressing experiences one can encounter. I emphasize that the aspects of yourself that seem irreparably damaged have the potential to heal. These exercises helped me regain my sense of worth and can also assist you. I understand that your trauma may have led you to blame yourself and feel hopeless. Letting go of this burden of shame, forgiving yourself, and approaching yourself with kindness and self-acceptance will guide you toward becoming whole again.

AFFIRMATIONS

Let's conclude with meaningful, compassionate, and loving affirmations. Repeat these and allow yourself to lovingly bathe in them, letting the words comfort and soothe your soul.

I am learning to be kind to myself.

I am allowed to celebrate the fact that I survived.

I will be patient and love myself as I heal.

Chapter Twelve

WILL I FOREVER BE BROKEN?

My scars tell a story. They are a reminder of times when life tried to break me but failed.

— STEVE MARABOLI

I am damaged goods, filthy, and unloveable. Pieces of me have been used, abused, and forever broken. How do I move forward, find my true self again, and know I can have a normal and happy life?

I t is common to harbor questions similar to the one from this client. It is entirely normal to feel shattered, hopeless, and forever broken after experiencing sexual assault(s).

It's time to talk about how to do the more profound work to heal from your sexual assault and start to live the life you deserve. I get that you just want to feel like your regular self again. You've been through intense trauma, and you're tired of feeling what you're feeling; you're tired of the pain and the struggle; you're tired of not feeling healthy, strong, empowered, or like your best self. It's hard not to let your experience define you, isn't it? Or perhaps you doubt if things will ever be ok regarding life, work, or relationships. Let's discuss how I tackle this task in my life and therapy practice.

EMDR THERAPY

EMDR therapy is my top pick. It's short for Eye Movement Desensitization and Reprocessing, a fantastic evidence-based trauma therapy that, if done right, won't re-traumatize you. When I participated in my own EMDR therapy, it was the only therapeutic approach that fundamentally altered my perception of myself and my trauma. This new perspective illuminated my experiences in a way that alleviated my shame and opened the door to self-love and self-worth.

EMDR therapy is a psychotherapy approach aimed at helping individuals process and overcome traumatic events by using bilateral stimulation techniques like eye movements or taps while focusing on the trauma. What I love most about this trauma therapy, as well as Somatic therapy listed below, is that you do not necessarily have to talk about the trauma to reprocess it. Therefore, getting retraumatized can be avoided.

Typically used for PTSD treatment, EMDR therapy can also benefit those dealing with anxiety, depression, or phobias, often rooted in unprocessed trauma or traumas. Traditional talk therapy can be limited because it primarily targets the logical and reasoning part of the brain. At the same time, trauma tucks away in the amygdala, which controls our instinctual and emotional responses. I recognized that my progress in talk therapy had plateaued, and I needed to delve into deeper issues of shame that were contributing to my perfectionism and dysfunctional relationships — which is where EMDR therapy played a crucial role.

EMDR therapy alleviated the emotional burden associated with my traumatic memories and enhanced my ability to manage it effectively. By integrating the traumatic event into my memory network, I was able to reduce the distress connected to those memories. This integration process established new pathways in my brain, enabling me to reposition the trauma appropriately and alleviate any emotional or physical discomfort it may have caused. As I released old thoughts and emotions, I created room for a renewed self-perspective.

In this kind of work, you can anticipate the release of common feelings such as guilt, shame, and self-blame. This process allows for the development of a new and healthier self-image. Furthermore, the physical sensations tied to your trauma are released, enabling the body to experience a revived sense of safety and pleasure.

DBT THERAPY

As much as I love EMDR therapy and think everyone can benefit from it, it may not be for you. Therefore, another helpful option is Dialectical Behavioral Therapy (DBT), ideal for managing emotions effectively. If mood swings, easy triggers, constant edginess, or hypervigilance sound familiar to you, DBT therapy can assist in grounding yourself emotionally and fostering healthier relationships.

DBT teaches skills for handling challenging emotions, enhancing relationships, and positively dealing with stress. Following the dialectical philosophy, it's all about finding a balance between acceptance and change.

The therapy includes individual sessions, group skill training, phone coaching, and therapist consultation. It has four main parts.

1. **Mindfulness:** Being aware of thoughts and feelings without judgment.
2. **Distress Tolerance:** Learning to deal with challenging situations without harmful actions.
3. **Emotion Regulation:** Managing intense emotions healthily.
4. **Interpersonal Effectiveness:** Enhancing communication skills and building healthy relationships.

DBT is also effective for treating other mental health issues like depression, anxiety disorders, eating disorders, and substance abuse. These mental health struggles are often rooted in unprocessed trauma.

To maximize the benefits of DBT, collaborate with a therapist who is trained in these techniques.

SOMATIC THERAPY

Another excellent evidence-based treatment is Somatic therapy, which focuses on the mind-body connection, suggesting that emotional issues may appear as physical symptoms. This therapy helps restore a safe connection between mind and body. This therapy highlights bodily sensations, movements, and experiences in the healing process. Somatic therapists help clients tune into their physical sensations and employ breathing exercises, movement, and body awareness to release tension, trauma, and stored stress. It can aid those coping with trauma, anxiety, depression, chronic pain, or other emotional and physical challenges. Somatic therapy is often used along with EMDR therapy to aid the body's release of stored trauma.

ACCEPTANCE AND COMMITMENT THERAPY

Acceptance and Commitment Therapy (ACT) helps individuals accept what they cannot control and commit to actions that enhance their quality of life. ACT acknowledges suffering as a natural part of the human experience; avoiding or controlling painful thoughts may lead to more distress—clients in ACT practice mindfulness, acceptance, and values-based action to foster psychological flexibility and resilience. The goal is for individuals to lead more meaningful lives by embracing their thoughts and feelings while moving toward their values and goals.

ACT is effective in treating various mental health issues such as anxiety, depression, chronic pain, and substance abuse—commonly used in individual therapy or group settings within behavioral health programs.

Finding the right therapist is crucial when considering any of these therapies. Like any relationship, it's essential to connect with someone you feel comfortable with—a person who creates a safe space where you can be authentic without fear of judgment. To ensure a good fit for individual therapy sessions, meeting with two or three therapists for a free consultation helps gauge the chemistry and choose the best match.

In group therapy, other survivors surround you, sharing their stories and providing comfort and support as you heal. It's an excellent setting to realize that you are not alone. Finding the therapy that suits you best is crucial no matter what you decide since everyone's journey is unique.

In therapy, you might be curious about what's ahead – like how long does this process take or if you'll still manage day-to-day stuff, and whether things will improve or worsen first. These are solid topics to chat about with your therapist. Just know that the timeline is flexible, and you'll adapt to a new kind of everyday living. Yup, sometimes it gets tougher before it gets easier.

Establishing a secure environment for therapy is crucial, where practices such as meditation and mindfulness can help you stay balanced outside of sessions. Before delving into trauma work, make sure you have the necessary coping mechanisms, resources (just like the ones I taught in the introduction), and trust in your therapist. This relationship is significant, so feeling secure during therapy and having tools for safety in between sessions is vital.

It's essential to feel capable of looking after yourself even when not in session. The goal is to avoid reaching a breaking point between sessions that might deter you from continuing therapy. It is appropriate to feel supported and equipped with tools and resources to manage any triggers that could come up. You may also receive referrals for additional resources like support groups or psychiatrists, depending on your struggle.

Therapy is hard work and can leave you feeling emotionally spent. It's super important to take it easy after a session and carve out time for self-care. Be intentional about not comparing your progress to others, as it could make you feel like you need to measure up. What counts is your power to heal at your speed and in your style.

It is time for a friendly warning. My warning is for you perfectionists out there. I'm not talking about those with the perfect home, grades, or looks. I'm talking to you who need to heal perfectly and quickly.

Perfectionism can sometimes mess things up and stop you from seeing things through. Treatment doesn't have a set timeframe. It all depends on how much you've been through, the kind of support you have, and how patient you are with the process. I often felt that I should have made more progress than I had. I questioned why past experiences continued to affect me, why I still struggled with my body image, and why, as a trained psychologist, I believed I ought to be more healed by this point (which only added to my feelings of shame!). It's common to just want it all over with so you can move on with life. But these mindsets only drag out the healing process that's bound to happen. Don't let perfectionism mess up your journey. Take it one day at a time, and remember, you're exactly where you need to be.

EXERCISES

Open your journal and answer the following questions:

1. Which of the therapies listed above piqued your interest? Why is that?
2. Are you aware of any perfection tendencies that might sabotage your journey? If so, how do you think perfection shows up in your life, and what are some consequences?
3. What is your goal of getting treatment/help?
4. Can you start to envision your life regarding what it can look like and feel like once you have healed from your trauma(s)?

AFFIRMATIONS

The following affirmations are special to me because they specifically address any shame you might have attached to seeking help or the heaviness you might feel along the healing journey. Let these affirmations soothe and inspire you!

I am allowed to ask for help.

I am right where I need to be.

I am healing my brokenness one day at a time.

Chapter Thirteen

HOW DO I SUPPORT A LOVED ONE WHO HAS EXPERIENCED SEXUAL ASSAULT?

I may not have all the answers, but I'll always be here to listen and support you.

— UNKNOWN

I didn't know how to respond or what to say to her. I simply didn't understand. I would give advice but get shouted at. Does she just want to vent? I have no idea what to do and am so afraid to lose her.

A re you watching someone you love going through a tough time? It spurs feelings of helplessness and frustration, right? You hate to see them in pain or pulling away from you. Ever wish you could make it all go away with a magic wand? Or, maybe you ignore the elephant in the room so you don't upset anyone, and they feel like you don't care. Sometimes, despite your best intentions, your efforts might backfire. And there's that fear of damaging the bond with your loved one. This chapter doesn't have any magic tricks up its sleeve, but it does give you some valuable insights on how to support a loved one who has been through a sexual assault.

As a friend or family member of someone who has experienced sexual assault, your support can play a crucial role in their healing process. Understanding the impact of sexual assault before diving into how to support a loved one is essential to understanding the profound impact that sexual assault can have on survivors. According to the Rape, Abuse & Incest National Network (RAINN), someone sexually assaults an American every 68 seconds! As has been stated throughout this book, survivors may experience a range of emotions, including fear, shame, guilt, anger, and confusion. There can also be physical symptoms such as insomnia, anxiety, depression, and post-traumatic stress disorder (PTSD). Witnessing someone you are close to exhibiting any of these signs can also evoke distress within you.

 My girlfriend has so much anxiety and is avoiding physical intimacy with me. I feel totally helpless in knowing what to do or how to support her. She is pushing me away and everyone else close to her. What does she need, and how can I stop feeling so rejected?

HOW TO SUPPORT A LOVED ONE

1. **Believe and Validate:** One of the most important ways to support a loved one who has experienced sexual assault is to believe them and validate their feelings. Many survivors face disbelief or skepticism from others, which can compound their trauma. By listening empathetically and affirming their experiences, you can provide a safe space for your loved ones to express their emotions. Be careful not to question your loved one with questions like, "Why did you go there in the first place?" "Why were you drinking so much?" "Why didn't you call me?" etc. These "why" questions tend to shame the victim, which is the last thing you want to do.

2. **Respect Their Autonomy:** It is crucial to respect your loved one's autonomy and empower them to make their own decisions regarding their healing journey. Avoid pressuring

them to disclose details of the assault or engage in activities that they are not comfortable with, i.e., reporting the incident or confronting the perpetrator. Encourage them to seek professional help, but ultimately let them take the lead in their recovery process. You can share your concerns and let your loved one go at their own pace.

3. **Provide Practical Support:** Practical support can be invaluable for a survivor of sexual assault. Offer to accompany them to medical appointments, therapy sessions, or support groups. Help them navigate the legal system if they choose to pursue legal action against their abuser. Assist with household tasks or childcare responsibilities to alleviate some of the stress they may be experiencing.

4. **Engage in Your Self-Care:** It is crucial to prioritize self-care, seek professional assistance, and establish a support network to effectively support your loved one. By ensuring you receive the support needed to manage your emotions, reactions, and coping strategies, you can maintain patience and emotional balance. A solid support system will enable you to remain present and support your loved one.

5. **Don't Take It Personally:** It is natural for there to be sudden shifts in the moods of a loved one who is a survivor of sexual assault. It is also common to notice alterations in intimacy and boundaries related to physical touch. Encourage open dialogue without judgment by asking what they need from you, expressing love and care, and being prepared for counseling. Remember not to internalize these changes as personal insults related to physical touch. These steps are all valuable in supporting their healing process.

Research indicates that social support plays a vital role in alleviating the adverse effects of trauma experienced by survivors of sexual assault. A strong support network can help survivors feel less isolated and more empowered to seek help. By believing in them, respecting their autonomy, and providing practical support, you can help your loved one navigate the challenging journey of healing and recovery. Respecting boundaries, practicing self-care, avoiding shaming language, and continuing your personal growth through therapy are key aspects of effectively supporting a survivor of sexual assault.

Remember that every survivor's experience is unique. By prioritizing patience, empathy, communication, and self-awareness throughout this journey, you can provide the best possible support for your loved one.

EXERCISES

1. Use a journal to explore your helplessness and desire to "fix" your loved one.
2. Write out ways to start taking care of yourself, whether by seeking professional help or creating a self-care routine so that your tank is complete and can be present for your loved one. Who do you need to have in your support network?
3. Be in touch with your own biases of how you might tackle this trauma vs your loved one. Can you embrace patience as your loved one is allowed to engage in healing in the way they feel is best?

AFFIRMATIONS

My empathy and understanding make a difference in my loved one's healing journey.

My ability to listen without judgment is a powerful gift to my friend.

My friendship/support is helping my loved one feel safe and supported.

Chapter Fourteen

DEFINITIONS: LET'S DEFINE WHAT SEXUAL ASSAULT IS

Trigger Warning!

Believe in yourself and all that you are. Know that there is something inside you that is greater than any obstacle.

— CHRISTIAN D. LARSON

If you're starting to explore the world of being a survivor of sexual assault, it's super important to understand some standard terms used in this sensitive area. Here are some key definitions to help you navigate the complexities of sexual assault, including terms like rape and molestation. Please be aware that these terms can be very triggering.

By equipping you with these words, I aim to help you articulate your experience effectively and empower you as you navigate your narrative toward healing. Upon completing this chapter, you will enrich your lexicon and deepen your comprehension of your unique narrative. Consider this journey a valuable learning experience where knowledge is the key to empowerment.

So, let's break it down. People often use terms related to sexual assault interchangeably, which is understandable. However, selecting words is essential, especially when describing one's experience. For example, saying "I hurt my foot" instead of "I broke my foot" creates different impressions, underscoring the importance of precise language in communication.

We hear the word "assault" a lot! What image comes to your mind when you hear that word? Let's define it and see if it changes your image or understanding of this widely used term.

> **Assault** involves physically attacking someone. Legally, three things make up an assault: intending harm or fear, the presence of fear or imminent danger, and actual or attempted physical contact.

> **Sexual assault** means sexual contact without the victim's consent. It ranges from unwanted touching to more serious acts like attempted rape or forcing sexual acts on someone.

> **Sexual molestation** falls under assault and refers to any sexual abuse towards an individual, especially minors. Molestation includes various acts like exposing genitals, taking explicit images, rape, or instigating sexual activities involving an abuser of children.

As we delve further into the nuances of sexual abuse and assault, it becomes apparent that understanding the specific classifications and implications of these acts is essential. This clarity includes recognizing the varying degrees of rape, from forced penetration without consent to situations involving unequal power dynamics or incapacity to give consent.

> **First-degree rape** is when a perpetrator forcibly penetrates a victim without their consent, disregarding the victim's autonomy and violating their boundaries.

> **In second-degree rape,** an adult takes advantage of a vulnerable individual's physical or mental state to engage in non-

consensual sexual contact, exploiting the power imbalance and causing harm to the victim.

An example of a power imbalance and exploitation of someone's physical or mental state in the context of sexual assault could involve a boss or supervisor taking advantage of their authority over an employee who is in a vulnerable position. For instance, the supervisor may pressure the employee into engaging in sexual activity by threatening their job security or career advancement, knowing that the employee may feel compelled to comply due to fear of losing their job. This situation demonstrates a clear power dynamic where the perpetrator uses their position of authority to exploit the victim's vulnerability and coerce them into non-consensual sexual activity.

> **Third-degree rape**, according to www.helpingsurvivors.org, entails engaging in non-consensual sexual intercourse with someone incapable of giving consent, such as a physically helpless individual, a minor, or someone with a mental disability. Remember that these definitions may vary slightly depending on your state, so it's advisable to visit www.helpingsurvivors.org for more detailed information tailored to your location.

No matter what degree of rape or attempted rape, all leave profound emotional scars on the victims.

Let's look at some definitions of rape and sexual assault even further. Remember that the aim is to help you feel empowered as you understand the significance of your own story and learn how to make sense of it.

TYPES OF SEXUAL ASSAULT AND RAPE

Understanding the different types of sexual assault is a critical step toward creating an inclusive and supportive environment for all survivors. Knowledge empowers you to recognize the varied forms of sexual violence, respond appropriately, and receive the proper support.

Here are some key types of sexual assault:

Unwanted Touching: This type of assault involves any non-consensual physical contact, such as groping or pinching, that is sexually motivated. It's a violation of personal boundaries and can occur in any setting.

Sexual Harassment: Sexual harassment encompasses unwelcome sexual advances, requests for sexual favors, and other verbal or physical harassment of a sexual nature. It can take place in work, school, or social environments, significantly affecting the victim's mental and emotional well-being.

Coerced Sexual Acts: An individual forces another person to engage in sexual acts against their will through threats, manipulation, or physical force in this form of assault. It strips the individual of their ability to make autonomous decisions about their sexual activity.

Cyber Sexual Assault: With the rise of digital platforms, cyber sexual assault has become increasingly prevalent. This can include non-consensual sharing of explicit images, sexual harassment online, or coercing someone into online sexual activities.

Acquaintance Rape: The perpetrator is known to the victim. It may be a friend, a coworker, or an intimate partner. Acquaintance rape shatters the trust and safety one feels in their connections and often complicates the survivor's healing process due to pre-existing relational dynamics.

Marital Rape: Marital rape, or spousal rape, happens within the bounds of marriage when one partner forces intercourse without the other's consent. This type of rape is more common than you might think. According to the National Intimate Partner and Sexual Violence Survey conducted by the Centers for Disease Control and Prevention (CDC), approximately 10.7% of women in the United States have experienced marital rape at some point in their lives. My personal opinion is that this is an underreported statistic. However, this statistic highlights the prevalence of this form of sexual violence within intimate relationships.

In any relationship, even marriage, it's crucial to understand and respect consent. Being married doesn't make one immune to the possibility of experiencing rape. When rape occurs within a marriage, it can leave the victims questioning their own experiences as valid instances of assault. In society, many people hold the common misconception that a spouse cannot commit rape. This belief can confuse the victim and make their recovery a lot more complex.

Heterosexual and Homosexual Rape: Both heterosexual and homosexual rape involve acts of sexual violence where consent is absent, but the dynamics can carry different societal perceptions and stigmas. In the context of heterosexual rape, people often frame it within the narrative of male aggression towards women, which, while significant, can overshadow the broader spectrum of sexual violence that affects individuals regardless of their gender or sexual orientation.

Homosexual rape, involving individuals of the same sex, confronts additional layers of stigma and misunderstanding. Survivors may face unique challenges in seeking help and support, fearing judgment not only for the assault but also for their sexual orientation, which can exacerbate feelings of isolation and distress.

Date Rape: Date rape occurs when a person, usually while on a social outing with the victim, disregards the necessity of consent and violates the false sense of security often associated with social or romantic settings. Understanding that consent is indispensable, and can be revoked at any point. You can prevent misconceptions, such as the belief that sex is expected at the end of a date or misinterpreting a person's enjoyment as an indication of forthcoming sexual activity, by acknowledging and respecting the concept of consent. Further discussion regarding consent is found in Chapter 2.

Stranger Rape: Stranger rape refers to a situation where the perpetrator is not known to the victim. This form of assault underscores the random and unpredictable nature of sexual violence, contributing to women's pervasive feelings of being constantly on guard, insecure, or at risk due to societal perceptions of them as the more vulnerable gender.

Statutory Rape: Statutory rape involves sexual activity with a person who is below the age of consent. This form highlights the importance of protecting minors from exploitation and identifying their incapability to give informed consent legally.

Understanding the complexities of sexual assault and its different manifestations is crucial in dealing with and comprehending your encounters. I get asked all the time if what someone experienced was sexual assault. Hopefully, this starts to bring clarity to your own story.

———

You will notice there are no exercises for this chapter. This chapter is merely an educational tool to have as a resource. But please engage with the following affirmations!

AFFIRMATIONS

Remember, you can use any or all of these on your healing journey. See which one vibes with you today, practice it, and change your affirmations as needed:

I can embrace my story, heal, and find liberation.

My story doesn't define me entirely; it shapes my identity into a resilient, empowered individual today.

My story matters.

AFTERWORD

In conclusion, "Unbroken: A Survivor's Journey After Sexual Assault" serves as a powerful testament to the resilience of the human spirit, bravely addressing the profound struggles that you and countless survivors endure. This book highlights the heart-wrenching questions that can trap you in a cycle of pain and despair, offering a space for reflection and understanding. It does not shy away from the heavy burdens of shame and self-blame that often weigh down your heart; instead, it compassionately unravels the complexities of your body's natural responses and the delicate nuances of consent, fostering a deeper understanding of your unique experience.

As you journeyed through its pages, you hopefully discovered a beacon of hope that guided you through the challenging terrain of relationships with abusers. The book empowers you to set healthy boundaries and emphasizes the importance of self-care, self-love, and self-compassion. In this transformative journey of healing, may you find solace and strength, knowing that you are not alone and that hope can indeed emerge from the shadows of your past.

I hope that as you immersed yourself in the words of this book, you felt the warmth of a loving embrace—a reminder that you are worthy of love, healing, and a brighter future. Now that you have completed this enlightening read, I encourage you to seek continued support. I have a wealth of resources available, and if you desire a more personal touch, either I or a member of my team would be honored to provide individual therapy sessions. We can explore your feelings and experiences in a safe and nurturing environment.

Additionally, if you wish to connect with others who share similar experiences, I invite you to reach out to me about the possibility of joining my sexual assault support group. This group fosters understanding, healing, and community, reminding you that you are never alone on this journey. Remember, you do not have to navigate this path in isolation; I am here to listen, guide, and walk alongside you as you reclaim your power and rebuild your life. You deserve all the compassion and understanding this world has to offer, and it is my privilege to be part of your journey toward healing and empowerment. Together, we can illuminate the path to a brighter tomorrow.

THANK YOU

I would like to extend my heartfelt thanks to all my clients, both past and present, for your trust and belief in me. Your courage in sharing your stories has been a profound source of inspiration.

To Red Thread Publishing, specifically Sierra Melcher, Mimi Rich and Erika Hull, thank you for your unwavering support and guidance throughout this journey. Everything from dotting my i's and crossing my t's to holding my hand and emotionally supporting me, your commitment to bringing this book to life has been invaluable.

To my beta readers, Abbey Goth, Dr. Cheryl Arutt, Jess Sveen, John Waites, Danielle Schreiber, and Angala Cramer, your insights and feedback have helped shape this work into what it is today. I am so blessed to have you all in my life and I am deeply grateful for your time and honesty.

To my son, Stephen: Your insights and our brainstorming sessions have been the spark that ignited this entire project!

To the love of my life, John: Your unwavering support and encouragement have been my greatest motivation. You are the first man in my life who truly sees me and shows me that love and care can be given without conditions. You inspire me to be a better person every day, and for that, I am forever grateful.

Finally, to my parents, thank you for your unwavering belief in me and your emotional and financial support throughout this process. Your encouragement has been priceless.

Together, you have all played a crucial role in allowing me to address this sensitive topic and share the painful truths that I hope will aid others on their healing journeys.

With deep appreciation,

Lesley

ABOUT THE AUTHOR

Lesley Goth is a passionate advocate for survivors of trauma and sexual assault, dedicated to fostering healing and empowerment through her work. With a background in trauma, including PTSD and CPTSD, as well as Eating Disorders, Anxiety, and Depression, she has spent over 20 years supporting individuals on their journey to recovery. As the author of "Unbroken: A Survivor's Journey After Sexual Assault," Lesley shares her insights and experiences to illuminate the path toward healing.

You can read more of Lesley's published works in **_Taboo: Stories that Can't Be Told_** on Amazon and at major book retailers. Lesley's chapter, _Breaking The Silence: Confronting The Taboo of Sexual Assault_, addresses the core issues of _Was it My Fault_, _Triggers_, and _Boundaries_.

In addition to her writing, Lesley offers individual and group therapy sessions, providing a safe and compassionate environment for survivors to explore their feelings and reclaim their lives. She is also a sought-after public speaker, sharing her message of hope and resilience at various events and workshops.

To further support survivors, Lesley provides a wealth of free resources including *Healing Foundations: A Resource To Healing After Sexual Assault*, self-care tips, and community support information. With a commitment to making a positive impact, Lesley invites you to connect and join her in this critical work of healing and transformation.

DO YOU HAVE A STORY?

Publish with Red Thread Books, an imprint of Red Thread Publishing.

We provide expert guidance to nonfiction authors through every stage of the publishing process. Visit **www.redthreadbooks.com** to learn more and connect with our team.

REVIEW THIS BOOK

Enjoyed *Unbroken*? Your feedback means the world! If the book resonated with you, inspired you, or offered something meaningful, we'd truly appreciate it if you left a review. Your feedback helps others discover the book—and it directly supports the author's work.